MW01491849

Those familiar with the lives of missionaries like Hudson Taylor, William Carey, David Livingston, and others are sometimes hesitant to believe that the God who performed miraculous acts through their ministries in past centuries is active and performing the same miracles today in the ministries of those individuals who are prepared to follow Him. The lives and ministry of Bill and Maria Wojtaszewski clearly demonstrate that God is still seeking to use those who are willing to be used.

Over a period of years, I've had the privilege to minister with Bill and Maria in such diverse locations as Siberia, China, Afghanistan, Bethlehem, and various countries of Eastern Europe and Latin America. I have seen how God has used them in a mighty way to bring glory to His name. I know this book will inspire every reader and help them to understand that God is prepared to use them if they are genuinely willing to trust Him.

RON OATES
Former Director of Humanitarian Operations,
CBN/Operation Blessing

I still remember the very first trip Bill and Maria made with our medical team and the major impact they made for the patients needing prescription glasses! For the first time, we were able to fill prescriptions immediately! It was amazing to see the dedication and love expressed to each person they helped. Bill and Maria impacted not only the people served but were a major blessing to all of the medical team members. They truly have servants' hearts. Their love for the Lord was infectious! Bill and Maria are a unique couple providing an ophthalmologic service unavailable to the vast majority of patients ministered to on the medical mission trips. Their stories of lives changed through their services are incredibly inspiring!

PAUL R. WILLIAMS, M.D.
Founder and President, International Health Care Network

One of the greatest and most rewarding seasons of my life was while serving as Director of Global Outreach for Jewish Voice Ministries International from 2009 until 2013. I had the unique privilege of working alongside some of the most selfless and devoted people I have ever met. We primarily served impoverished Jewish communities located in Ethiopia, Zimbabwe, and India. During our medical outreach campaigns, it was not uncommon for our teams to treat between 7,000 and 9,000 patients in a single week. When reflecting on the people and leaders on our teams, Bill Wojtaszewski stands apart as one of the great heroes of our outreaches. While older than most on our trips, Bill and his wife Marie proved that the rules of age didn't apply to them. Without a doubt, they outpaced individuals half their age. Bill and Marie served as part of our optometry team.

Over the years, they became fixtures on more outreaches than I can count. They worked with tireless resilience and were consumed by the mission to serve the precious people that God placed directly in front of them. As part of their assignment, they would prepare for each outreach by ordering thousands of pairs of glasses in the United States, would carefully inventory and package the cargo, and, finally, would personally oversee the successful transport of the large supply of reading glasses from their home all the way to the clinic site.

Bill and Marie were motivated by God's love. They longed to return and reconnect with those they had served. They rejoiced that God's love was being released in hearts and homes because of the sacrifices they continued to make. Yet, not only did Bill and Marie help bring relief to the physical blindness of their patients, they also became agents of God's power to love, touch, heal, and bring relief to spiritual blindness of the precious people they served.

DR. JONATHAN GANNON
President, Southwestern Assemblies of God University
American Indian Campus

As CEO of Jewish Voice Ministries, I meet many wonderful volunteers that serve with our outreach programs. Bill Wojtaszewski has to be one of the most dedicated and sincere volunteers that I have ever encountered. His story of miraculous events in his life recorded in *Sure Enough* . . . leading to his eventual call, embodies the story of so many lives in the Scriptures where God had numerous detours for those He called to serve. This book should encourage anyone who feels that their trials could never lead to an eventful life of such sweet Christian service as Bill has experienced. I experienced some of these sweet stories with Bill on our mission trips. This is a must-read if you need to see the power of Yeshua—both in ordinary lives and in medical missions.

JONATHAN BERNIS, CEO
Jewish Voice Ministries International

SURE ENOUGH

MIRACLES FROM WORLD WAR TO WORLD MISSIONS

WASYL "BILL" WOJTASZEWSKI

LUCIDBOOKS

Sure Enough: Miracles From World War to World Missions

Published by Lucid Books in Houston, TX
www.LucidBooks.com

paperback ISBN: 978-1-63296-536-3
hardback ISBN: 978-1-63296-537-0
eBook ISBN: 978-1-63296-538-7

Special Sales: Most Lucid Books titles are available in special quantity discounts. Custom imprinting or excerpting can also be done to fit special needs. Contact Lucid Books at Info@LucidBooks.com

This book is dedicated to my wife, Maria, who has been by my side on each missionary journey, and to my family who has supported, encouraged, and prayed for us each step of the way.

Special Thanks

I would like to extend a special thanks to Dr. Mark Eanes and his wife, Jo, for making this book possible. I would also like to thank everyone who encouraged me to document my stories before they escape my memory.

Contents

Foreword

Listening to Bill tell one of his stories would make anyone wish for a photographic memory, and listening to him tell the story again makes it even better.

I have known Bill as a precious friend and fellow servant on the medical mission field for 23 years, first meeting him and Maria, his wife, on a mission trip to Russia in 1999. He is one of those giants in my life who has impacted my Christian walk—simply from being around him. I have observed him walk into what most would consider to be tense situations, and I have watched as the atmosphere in the room changed with just his presence and his smile.

Bill's command of opticianry skills is unmatched. I have been in the field of eye care for 38 years, but I have only met *one* Bill. While many accept accolades for mission work, Bill humbly knows that he was simply called to do the work. He answered that call, and he will tell you his life has never been the same.

His stories reach back to early childhood memories of the miraculous sparing of his life during World War II. He tells how the gospel was shared with his parents while they were in a concentration camp and how this seed grew into Christianity, resulting in a unique bridge for his gradual migration to the United States.

Taking the journey with Bill through this book will encourage believers. It can bring life and hope to aspiring missionaries who face seemingly impossible obstacles, fearing it will never be. His testimony may even birth new believers as they see the magnificence of Bill's God, and as they understand that He is available to them as well.

And as for his stories . . . well, just read each one a few times. You will be blessed.

—Mark J Eanes, MD
Medical Director, Heaven In Sight Missions

PART I

Wasyl "Bill" Wojtaszewski

Go ye therefore, and teach all nations, baptizing them in the name of the Father, and of the Son, and of the Holy Ghost Teaching them to observe all things whatsoever I have commanded you: and, lo, I am with you always, even unto the end of the world. Amen.

—Matt. 28:19–20 (KJV)

CHAPTER ONE

It Just So Happened That

The LORD will watch over your coming and going both now and forevermore.

—Ps. 121:8

Humble Beginnings

I was born to Polish parents in 1937 in a little town called Kortschitzka, just outside Pinsk, Poland. We lived in a small farmhouse, which my father had built little by little. This was because, during World II, building materials were hard to come by, and finding money to buy them was even harder. Despite this, he managed to complete the house when I was about four years old.

We lived on the border of a large swamp—one in a series of swamps that joined together to form a border separating Germany from Russia. A faction of rebel fighters known as "Partisans" operated out of these swamps under the command of a Russian general. These supposedly fierce fighters were nothing more than bums who did not want to work. They were not particularly organized and not very well-funded. In a group of ten, maybe two of them would carry rifles, and the other eight would use knives and sticks for weapons. They were cowardly and came out most often at night to hunt for food or anything else they could get their hands on.

I remember many a summer night when we were forced to sleep outside in the bushes, watching them come and take whatever we had. We tried to hide everything and bury our most precious items to keep the Partisans from taking them. During the day, a German army patrol often came around to look for the Partisans. The patrol usually stopped at our farm because it was the last one before the swamps, and they did not want to go into the swamps. Their reluctance was more than likely due to common knowledge that if you went into the swamps without knowing your way around, you probably would not come out alive.

One night in 1941, we were awakened by voices outside our house, banging loudly on the door. My father opened the door and there stood six or seven men—Partisans. I was five years old, and my life was about to be drastically changed. They barged past my father and told my mother to "get ready" because they were taking both of them, but they were going to leave my little sister and me behind—alone. My sister was only three years old, and my mother tried desperately to hold on to her, but one of the Partisans ripped her from my mother's arms and threw her to the floor. I did not know why or where they were taking my parents, and my sister and I spent the night alone. The next morning my uncle and cousin came to check on us because word had traveled that several of the houses had been robbed in the middle of the night. As my uncle suspected, he found us there, alone and scared. He took us to his home in the village, which was about three-quarters of a mile away.

Fearing the Worst

During the first week at our uncle's home, we heard nothing from our parents. The second week passed and then the third, and still, we heard nothing. Either no one knew what had happened to them, or they were too afraid to say. My uncle had four children, and his house was very small, so my sister and I slept under the kitchen table. We usually went to bed when the sun went down because we had no electricity.

One evening at dusk when we were preparing to turn in for the night, we heard a horse and rider approach the house. When the knock on the door came, my uncle answered. I could hear a man's voice speaking, but I could not see him from where I was (under the table). I heard him tell my uncle he had seen my parents hanging in the woods, dead. After the man left, my uncle checked on us, and I pretended to be asleep, so he assumed we did not hear the news. I remember grabbing tightly to the table leg, crying and crying until I finally fell asleep. From that time on, everyone believed my parents were dead but, sure enough, our God had another plan. My father lived to tell me the story of what had *really* happened to them when I was about 10 years old.

The Partisans liked to hold their own version of "court," so my parents were tried and found guilty of collaborating with the Germans, and they were sentenced to execution. How idiotic that was! For one thing, my father was accused of being a spy when he did not even know how to sign his name. For another, when a German army patrol came to the farm to hunt for Partisans, unlike the Partisans who had only sticks and knives and maybe a rifle or two, their soldiers were heavily armed. My father could not have prevented the Germans from coming in no matter how much he might have wanted to. There was no way he could have told them, "No, I don't want you to stop here—get out!" Nevertheless, the ignorant Partisans condemned them, and they were sentenced to be executed.

My parents were held about 20 to 30 kilometers from our house in a town called Mohro. The rebels had taken over a farm outside of town and made it their local headquarters where about forty-five men were stationed. The prisoners, including my mother and father, were being held in a little house outside the farm. Once my parents had appeared in the Partisan's "court" in Mohro, their papers and transcripts were sent to the rebels' main headquarters in Molodechno, where the decision would be made regarding their fate. It took a long time for their papers to arrive at headquarters because the Germans were bombing the area heavily, making travel extremely dangerous. Finally, after almost six weeks, the papers arrived back in Mohro with a final verdict of "execution."

Faithful to the End

> *I have fought the good fight, I have finished the race, I have kept the faith. Now there is in store for me the crown of righteousness which the Lord, the righteous Judge, will award to me on that day—and not only to me, but also to all who have longed for His appearing.*
>
> —2 Tim. 4:7–8

Late one evening in November, as it was getting colder and the water was beginning to freeze, four men came to the little house where my father and mother were being held. "Get ready; we are going to take you home!" one of the men said. My mother started to cry because she knew what that meant. The Partisans' method of execution was a particularly brutal one. They were known for taking people into the woods and cutting off their hands and feet, then arms and legs, and even hanging women by their breasts. My parents had heard all about these murders. In fact, two days prior, they had witnessed the execution of one of the local Baptist pastors who had been in the same jail with them. But he was not just any pastor. It just so happened that this man was a giant of the faith, and each day he had been faithful to tell my parents about their need for salvation. Although my father did not acknowledge faith in Christ at that time, the seed was planted very strongly. Praise God for a man who was faithful and obedient to the end! It is this kind of faithfulness that can be used by God to change the eternal destination of one man, resulting in the salvation of an entire family, and leaving a legacy of generations of faithful Christians!

It seemed all hope was lost, but God was still in control. Just before the executioners took my parents away, another man came into the building and said, "Look, it's late so let's have supper, and then we'll take care of them." The executioners must have thought it was a good idea because instead of taking my parents, they left them to be watched by only one man—a man who had become crippled when he lost one of his legs fighting the Germans. Sure enough, as soon as the four men left to eat supper, the crippled man sat down by the stove and fell fast asleep. Later, my father would say it was as if "God put a sleep on him." My father took the man's rifle and would have killed him if my mother had not stopped him. Instead, he told my mother to take the bucket to the well in the middle of the yard (it was not uncommon for prisoners to be sent to the well to draw water). He told her to drop the pail as soon as she reached the well and then run in the direction of town just as fast as she could. He told her that he would follow shortly, and that is exactly what they did.

They ran for maybe five or six hundred yards before they came upon a group of Partisans returning from town. As God would have it, they did not recognize my parents right away because they had been held in a different house; not all the Partisans knew the faces of all the prisoners. They ordered my father to stop and then demanded to know where he was going. My father later said it was as if God had given him the words: "We're going home." It just so happened that German airplanes had bombed the area earlier in the afternoon, and people had been scattered everywhere, so it made sense to the rebels that my parents were in this group of people trying to return home. After all, they *were* going in the direction of the town. My parents continued in the direction they were going—slowly at first, then faster and faster until they were running as fast as they could! Unfortunately, just before they were out of the Partisans' sight, they heard the alarm from the farm blaring—the alarm signaled there were escaping prisoners. The rebels immediately turned and began to chase my parents.

In the Dead of Night

> *Our God is a God who saves; from the Sovereign Lord comes escape from death.*
>
> —Ps. 68:20

With the advancing cold, some of the water in the swamp had turned to ice, and a heavy fog had rolled in. They were running just as hard as they could, and my father said to my mother, "We will keep going straight toward town, but once we get into the fog, we will turn 90 degrees." This turned out to be a good plan because the Partisans believed my parents were still running toward town, so they continued in that direction. They were not aware that my parents had gone in another direction, quietly slipping off into the darkness and disappearing from sight.

My parents reached the river Pina after traveling for about two hours on foot, there they found a floating bridge that led to a German outpost on the opposite side of the river. My father knew that the bridge would be pulled to the outpost at sunset as an effective way to prevent anyone from crossing the river in the dark. He also knew that if anyone tried to swim to the bridge, the Germans would shoot first and ask questions later, so this made swimming to the bridge out of the question. Instead, he decided to go about two kilometers upriver to his cousin's house which, unfortunately, was *also* on the German side of the river.

Without the availability of a boat, my father was forced to come up with another plan to cross the river. The Germans had placed telephone poles along the shore, but the Partisans had knocked several of them down. My father and mother pulled a couple of poles together, tied them with telephone wires, and planned to use them as a makeshift raft. They soon discovered this desperate plan would not work for a couple of reasons. First, although the river was deep, the current was not strong, and this had resulted in a thin layer of ice forming on top of the water, making forward progress almost impossible. Next, as the contraption began to sink from their combined weight, they discovered it would not carry two people in the *best* of circumstances, much less in this one. My father was forced to tell my mother to swim back to the riverbank and hide in the bushes, and from there, she watched my father continue to fight his way across the icy river. As she hid in the bushes—wet and shivering and afraid—she heard the voices of angry Partisans coming nearer and nearer. These were the same Partisans they had encountered earlier, and they were still searching for them. My mother stayed as quiet and still as she could for what seemed like forever until she eventually heard one of the men say, "There is nobody here!" She was relieved when they finally went on their way, still in search of them. She remained in the woods, waiting for my father to come back for her. She was wet, cold, and afraid.

My father continued on his journey. It was late at night when he finally reached the house that belonged to his cousin. When he knocked on the window, it frightened his cousin, who demanded to know who was there. "It's me, Steve!" my father yelled through the window. His cousin replied, "No! You are dead!" and he refused to open the door. People in that culture believed in ghosts and supernatural things such as that so, naturally, he did not want to open the door. My father pleaded with him to come out and help him: "I am alive! My wife is across the river, and I have to somehow reach her; please help me!" His cousin peeked through a crack in the curtains and saw that my father was a real person. Once he was finally convinced that my father was not a spirit, he helped him build a bigger raft to cross the river, and my father was able to go back and rescue my mother who had been waiting—still wet, cold, and afraid.

CHAPTER TWO

We've Come This Far

See, I am doing a new thing! Now it springs up; do you not perceive it? I am making a way in the wilderness and streams in the wasteland.

—Isa. 43:19

Right People, Right Places

Once safely on the other side, my parents had no choice but to surrender themselves to the German Army outpost by the bridge. The Germans did not believe them when they explained what had happened to them. My parents were told that they would have to wait until the main headquarters at Pinsk could be contacted, that the soldier's "hands were tied" to do anything before then. They wanted headquarters to tell them what to do with my parents because they were not sure how to handle the situation.

My mother told the Germans, "Look, I have a brother who is on the police force in Pinsk. You can check my story." (It just so happened that her brother had been placed on the police force in Pinsk before the German occupation there. When the Germans came in, they told everyone, including my uncle to stay put at their duties. He was to remain at his post as a policeman, but he was to be under German control.) The Germans were very skeptical of my mother, saying, "How do we know? You might just be spies trying to find out what is going on here." Finally, they called Pinsk to verify my mother's story and confirmed that my uncle was indeed on the police force.

When my uncle heard about my parents' capture, he appealed to the German Major at headquarters who had, "coincidentally," come once or twice a week with a patrol to our farm in the past. He said to the major, "Do you remember the family with the farm at the edge of the swamps? Those people are my sister and brother-in-law. They were arrested by the rebels but were able to escape by the bridge, and now they have come here to try to get help." The appeal worked, and the major gave the okay over the phone to give my parents a pass to take the train from the outpost to Pinsk.

Human Shields

> *Yea, though I walk through the valley of the shadow of death, I will fear no evil: for thou art with me; thy rod and thy staff they comfort me.*
>
> —Ps. 23:4 (KJV)

The train station was about two kilometers from the outpost. When my parents finally reached the station, the first train to arrive was a military one. They were told that they could not ride in a regular passenger wagon with the soldiers; instead, they were to ride in one of the three cargo wagons at the front of the locomotive. The Partisans were known to plant land mines on the tracks to sabotage the trains, so as a cushion, the Germans had filled each of the front wagons a quarter of the way with sand. The idea was that these wagons would hit the mines first, preventing damage to the locomotive and the rest of the train behind them. My parents were made to ride in one of the front wagons.

Travel to the first station was uneventful, and when the train stopped, the conductor came to their wagon. He told them they were approaching an area ahead that was suspicious, and many trains had encountered land mines there. He told them they would be safer at the back of the train, and he sent them to ride in the caboose. My father and mother who were tired, hungry, and cold gratefully followed the conductor's instructions and went to the back of the train. On the floor of the old-fashioned caboose, they found crusts that had been broken off some old bread (as is common in Europe). They were already eating dried crusts off the floor as the train was leaving the station.

The train had not been traveling for more than five minutes before it hit a mine, and the explosion knocked them off their feet! The train came to an abrupt stop, and the soldiers jumped off to survey the damage. My father and mother got up off the floor and looked to see what had happened. Sure enough, they found the first three cargo wagons were now nothing more than "charred toothpicks," as my father put it. These were the same wagons my parents had been riding in no less than ten minutes earlier. The train was forced to remain there for many hours while the track was repaired, and then they were on their way. Eventually, the train reached Pinsk, and the only option for my parents was to report immediately to the German headquarters. There they were questioned all day about what happened, how it happened, and how they ended up there. Once again, the Germans did not want to take their word for it and were suspicious that my parents were spies. Eventually, they were released into the care of my mother's brother, the policeman, in Pinsk.

Bill's uncle who helped protect him (left) and Bill's father (right) years later after the family immigrated to the United States.

During all this time, my sister and I had remained at my uncle's house, still believing my parents were dead. Finally, my uncle decided he did not want us in their home after my parents were declared dead because he feared the Partisans would come back soon to execute us. He told his younger brother who was only 16 years old at the time, "Why don't you take care of them?" My uncle was afraid that something bad would happen to his family if we stayed, so he sent us to our home near the swamps in the care of our 16-year-old uncle.

CHAPTER THREE

Perseverance in Hardship

For we live by faith, not by sight.

—2 Cor. 5:7

A Father's Protection

Back in Pinsk, my father decided to ask permission to go with the next German patrol to the area where our farm was located. They were hesitant at first, so he asked to speak to the commander who he knew had come to our village in the past. Sure enough, the commander recognized him! "Oh yes, I remember you; we used to stop at your house," he said. My father explained to the commander what had happened and said he would like to go back with the patrol to get his children. After all this time, my father still believed in his heart that we were there. The commander told him he would check with his superiors and then let him know. A couple of days later, the commander told my father that a patrol would be leaving in three days and would be going as far as the farm. He agreed to let my father go on one condition: "Your wife has to remain at the headquarters in case anything happens. If there is any trick or if anything happens to the patrol, she will be executed." My parents agreed to the commander's terms.

The very day before the Germans were scheduled to patrol the farms, someone from the Partisan camp found out about the patrol, so the rebels came to the village and ordered everyone into the woods. Just before the capture of my parents, everyone had received orders from the Partisans to dig foxholes in the swamp, and each family had their own little foxhole they were to hide in. The rebels ordered the entire village to evacuate their farmhouses because they had gotten news that the German patrol was coming and that my father was with them. And that is how we discovered my father was alive—when we heard that he was coming for us! Sure enough, the next day he came to the village and found only a very few people remained—those who were either crippled or old and unable to evacuate. He asked those who had been left behind where everyone else had gone. Specifically, he wanted to know where his children were! They explained to him the order had come from the Partisan's camp to evacuate everyone to their foxholes. This alerted my father that the Partisans were probably waiting for them, so he warned the German commander that it would be safer for his patrol to leave the area to avoid an ambush. He pointed out to the commander some tight points here and there further down the road where the Partisans might use heavy machine guns and try to cut them off on either side of the path.

It was early in the morning, and my sister and I were sitting in a foxhole alone, unaware of what was unfolding. Suddenly, we heard a commotion and then gunshots started ringing out all around us. We did not know what was going on, but we stayed inside the foxhole as we had been told. Suddenly, my father appeared! He was crying tears of joy as he grabbed us from the foxhole, shouting, "Let's go, let's go! We're going home!" A fight had broken out when the Germans came across a foxhole where a couple of Partisans had been hiding out. Naturally, the Germans had more ammunition than was necessary and they were shooting carelessly in every direction. The frightened villagers ran away into the woods, including my 16-year-old uncle who had been taking care of us. My father called out to him and tried to get him to go back with us, but he was nowhere to be found. We were not allowed time to search for him either; we had to return with the Germans.

We were placed in a wagon drawn by a horse, and my father put us behind piles of hay to protect us from flying bullets as much as he could. Even during the retreat, there was sporadic shooting, and bullets were whizzing by way too close for comfort! Just as my father had predicted, the Partisans tried to cut off the patrol at the very place he had warned them about, and there the fighting was *very* heavy. Eventually, we reached our old farmhouse along with the motorized vehicles the Germans had left there because they had been unable to proceed into the swamp with them. They put us into one of the trucks and we sped off. After we had gone a mile or two down the road, we looked back and saw heavy smoke rising into the sky, coming from what once had been our farmhouse—the house my father had so patiently built with his hands. The Partisans had followed us, and they had burned our home to the ground the minute we left.

A Mother's Joy

Once we were safely on the road, the commander communicated with headquarters; he told them that everything had gone fine and that they had retrieved the children and were on their way back to Pinsk. Sure enough, it had been a miracle from God that amidst all the heavy fighting, not one soldier had been wounded! With this news, the Germans released my mother. We arrived at the plaza where headquarters was located just as she was coming out of the building. When she saw us, she ran to us and embraced us. Now, it was her turn to cry tears of joy!

We stayed with my uncle (the policeman) in Pinsk for a day or so, but his apartment was so small there was barely enough room for him, much less four more people. Once again, he petitioned the German government—this time for some form of temporary housing for us. They gave us the use of a small house in Pinsk, which had belonged to a Jewish family. It was situated behind a storefront that the Germans had taken over and turned into a depository of various army items. For almost a year they allowed us to call the little house our home.

A Concentration Camp and a Close Call

> *I will bless those who bless you, and whoever curses you I will curse.*
>
> —Gen. 12:3a

Things were not going very well for Germany on the war front. Eventually, one of the officials came to us and said, "It looks like we are going to have to retreat soon. What is your position? Do you want to stay, or do you want to go to Germany?" We had no choice but to sign up and go voluntarily to Germany.

The day finally came for our departure from Pinsk, Poland—destination: Germany (although no one knew exactly where). The year was 1942, and I cannot remember the exact month, but I remember it was cold and that snow was on the ground. When we arrived at the station, we were put onto cargo trains that looked exactly like the ones from the movie, Dr. Zhivago. It was a long train, and many of the cars had been locked from the outside because they housed prisoners, those who were being taken by force to Germany. Since our family was one of only a couple of families going to Germany voluntarily, the doors to our car were left unlocked. We were last in the convoy, and it just so happened that food for the entire train was stored in our car. In one of the corners were dozens of kielbasas about the size of a salami (approximately two feet long). We had the freedom to eat as much and as often as we liked.

When the train stopped at the end of each day, we were sad to see the meager portions thrown through the windows of the other cars where the prisoners were being held. The water had been stored in our car too, but unfortunately, it was gone after only a couple of days. I will never forget the sound of the prisoners in the other cars as they screamed and begged for water. Each time the train stopped, we were permitted to leave our car to go to the bathroom and get water. The prisoners, however, were not able to get out as their cars remained locked from the outside. Obviously, while our situation was far from luxurious, it certainly could have been worse. There was no furniture in our cart, but there was a straw floor. The weather was bitter cold, but we had a barrel in the middle of the car which we tried to keep continuously burning with wood. It was warm enough next to the barrel, but if you walked away only a little bit, the cold was intolerable. It did not help matters much that the wagon was full of holes.

The train served dual purposes. During the day, it was parked strategically, usually on bridges, in an effort to keep the bridges from being bombed by the Allies. Once again, my parents found themselves being used as human shields to protect the bridges and other key locations, only this time their children were placed at risk too. Traveling at night, the train continued for approximately a week until we finally pulled off the mainline and found ourselves in the countryside. Here, the travel was extremely slow, but finally, the train slowed to a stop at a large gate, which was flanked by what seemed like endless barbed wire extending in both directions.

As the train slowly pulled into the compound, reality set in, and we realized we were in a concentration camp. Crying and screaming could be heard from the terrified prisoners in the other cars. We were told to get out of the train, and our car—the last car—was the first to be unloaded. They took us to the main building while trying to reassure us, "Don't worry, don't worry, " but everyone was scared and crying just knowing that we were in a concentration camp. We were taken to the showers and told to undress, and our clothing was taken; we were not allowed to dress again until our clothing had undergone a "disinfection" process. We were given a little bit of hot soup with bread and then told to go back to the cars. It was not until we were back in the cars that we began to relax a little. I guess you could say it was somewhat of a scary moment.

It was starting to get dark by the time they pulled our car out of the camp and began to unload the cars that had held the prisoners. We were taken to wait at the nearest station, which was not far—maybe a half-hour or so away—and we waited for morning to come. It was not until morning finally dawned that we realized how much shorter the train had become, and how many of the cars had been left in the concentration camp . . . along with all the souls who had been riding in them. I was around five years old at the time, and although I have tried to remember the name of the camp, I cannot. My father never told me which one it was, either.

CHAPTER FOUR

Sojourners

Is anything too hard for the Lord?

—Gen. 18:14a

Miraculous Healing

The journey into Germany took about two weeks. Once again, we only traveled at night, parking the train over bridges and other places during the day to shield these areas from being bombed. When we finally arrived at one of the stations (I cannot remember the name), they told everyone in our car to take our luggage (whatever we had with us) and get out. It took a couple of hours to process the necessary paperwork before my family was finally told to climb onto a horse-drawn wagon. A very rough-looking, rough-spoken man told us we would be going with him. He was not a kind man, and he spoke roughly to everyone, not just to us. We had no choice but to go with this man, so we rode with him on his wagon until we reached the outskirts of a town called Kulbach. We arrived at his farm, and he told us this is where we would work and live. We unloaded our luggage, and he showed us to what was to be our new home. It consisted of one room with three beds—one for me, one for my sister, and one for my parents.

After a couple of days at our "new home," I developed a low-grade fever and began to feel ill. Within a week or so, I was bedridden with a fever so high I fell into a semiconscious state. The farmer would not allow my mother to come and check on me during the day, but she became so worried that occasionally she would ignore his demands and sneak in to check on me. When the farmer caught her leaving work to come see me, he was very rough with her and yelled at her to get back to work. I am not sure how many days I was in this condition before two Catholic nuns came to visit. My father later told me of how the nuns checked me all over to try to find the cause of the fever, but then they just stood there without saying anything. They did not know what was wrong with me either. The nuns came to check on me every day for a while until finally, they said, "You have to get him to a doctor." Unfortunately, there was no doctor to be found. The little town nearby had once supported two doctors, but they had long since been taken to the war front. The trip to and from the nearest city where a doctor could be found would take practically an entire day by horse and carriage. The only other option was to take a bus which was scheduled to go to the city and then return two days later. If we were going to make this trip, we also had to have signed permission from the farmer, and the document had to be stamped by the town official. Of course, the farmer refused to permit my parents to go. For three weeks I lay there, unconscious with a high fever, and no one know what was wrong or what was going to happen to me.

The nuns continued to visit, trying to give me water and feed me soup. During one of these visits, they found me lying on my left side and noticed a little spot of what looked like pus draining onto the pillow. They looked in my left ear and could see that my entire ear was full of pus, so much that it was draining out of my ear and onto the pillow. What we did not know was this: When we were on the train and sleeping on straw, one of the wheat grains had found its way into my ear. Because the ear is a warm and humid environment, the grain germinated and started to grow. The wheat germ could not break through, so it grew in the other direction—the direction of my eardrum. The resulting infection had gone untreated and had led to a high fever and loss of consciousness, becoming potentially deadly. The nuns ran quickly and called a pharmacist, who came and brought some equipment with him. Sure enough, the pharmacist was able to clean my ear, and after about two days my fever subsided. Thank God!

Vengeance Denied

It was almost another week before I was able to get up and walk. Although I still needed a lot of attention as I recovered, the farmer *still* would not allow my mother to leave her duties to check on me. He followed her on one occasion when he realized she was sneaking out to see me. He grabbed her by the collar and told her to get out, and then he hit her! There was nothing that could be done about it, however. He was a member of the Nazi party, and he *was* the law. Some of the neighbors became aware of what was happening there (probably hearing it from the nuns) and went to the German authorities on our behalf to ask them to transfer us. Finally, somehow, someone obtained permission from the authorities to have us transferred. One of the nearby farmers took us to the higher authorities in the city to make it official. The cruel farmer heard about this and followed us to the city. He was so angry when he found us that he yelled all sorts of insults and threats. As a matter of fact, he struck my mother again—this time twice—in the face! My father was forced to stand by and watch it happen because if he retaliated, he would surely be sent to a concentration camp along with the rest of his family. I cannot imagine how difficult that must have been for him.

Somehow, by God's grace, another farmer requested us, and the authorities permitted us to live and work at her farm. Our new farmer was an elderly lady named Mrs. Lorba; her husband and two sons had been killed in the war. She had a huge farm, but she only had one employee to help her run it, and he was a crippled man. From the very first day, our lives at her farm were much better. At least she fed us well and took care of us. After a short while of my father working for her, the farm was starting to get back into shape. She was very appreciative and became even more kind to us.

An Exploding Sky

> *Be strong and courageous. Do not be afraid or terrified because of them, for the Lord your God goes with you; he will never leave you nor forsake you*
>
> —Deut. 31:6

The day came for us to go into the city to finalize the paperwork. We went into a building but soon were told to go back outside because the other farmer was waiting for us (the previous farmer who had been so cruel). However, we found an even greater threat awaited us outside. It was an air raid! Everyone was scattering around, panicking, and running to find shelters. We had no shelter to run to and no idea where to go, so we just stayed by the building and prayed we would escape with our lives. One of the bombs practically demolished the building across the street. It just so happened that the very front of the building was still standing . . . the part of the building that had protected us from flying debris and stones that were being thrown in our direction. This was yet another miracle God allowed so that we would survive that awful place.

During the next few weeks, we received many warnings that air raids would take place at night. Because of this, we often slept in fields outside, away from the buildings. This was especially important at our farmhouse because it was unusually large, and large buildings were the ones most often targeted. One morning we awakened to the sound of vehicles in the yard. The Germans had sent men to paint a big red cross on the roof of the farm to signify the building as a hospital. However, it was not used as a hospital but became a headquarters for German operations. They even parked ambulances around it to complete the deception and keep the Americans from bombing it. This went on for a couple of weeks before a rumor was spread that the American forces were getting closer, so the Germans moved on. We did not know whether the rumor was true or not because we were not officially allowed to listen to the radio. My father occasionally listened anyway when the old lady went to the store to buy supplies. She was crippled, and it took her a long time to go the three kilometers each way to the store and back, so he took advantage of the time she was gone.

An "Attractive" Cannon

One day we watched as the Germans brought a cannon into the nearby town. They tried to camouflage it by placing it into a hole they had prepared on the south side of town. They aimed it toward the main road, which led into town from the northwest. They assumed that the Americans were going to come from that direction, and they expected to stop them with this one cannon. It turned out that their assumption was not accurate because a couple of days after that, one of the small American reconnaissance planes flew low over the town and discovered the cannon.

The very next day, my father and sister and I were on the east side of town plowing a piece of land that belonged to the farmer when a convoy of about five or six German trucks carrying supplies (mostly food) passed by on the road next to the field. Suddenly and out of nowhere, three American fighter planes swooped down and began to shoot at the convoy as they moved out of town and onto the open road. My father was plowing on a small hill, and the airplanes flew so close to us that shells from the machine guns fell all around us. I was sitting by the road near the carriage with my sister, while my father was deeper in the field with the horse and plow. I watched in horror as one of the planes came near him and dipped down so close to the ground that I thought it would crash on top of him. He fell to the ground, but he was unharmed.

Meanwhile, the town was being bombed. It just so happened that the reconnaissance plane that had been flown over the day before had been shot with the cannon, but had managed to make it back over to the American side. This turned out to be a mistake on the part of the Germans because, after that, the sky became black with American fighter planes. My father was still lying there on the ground when I grabbed my little sister and we started running toward the farm. Unfortunately, we had to cross town, which was burning, to get to our farm on the other side. There was a scary moment when machine gunfire cut in front of us and opened a large hole in the asphalt, so we ran into the bushes on the side of the road and did not stop until we made our way into town.

Ironically, the first farm on the edge of town belonged to the man we had previously worked for, the cruel German. A bomb fell on his farm just as we reached it. I often look back in awe of God's miraculous provision and protection throughout my lifetime, and this was one of those times. It just so happened that the bomb fell from high in the sky into the smallest and most unlikely target . . . a deep well in the farmer's yard! Despite falling into the well, when the bomb exploded it opened a deep crater in the ground, approximately the size of a house, but we were spared. The blast threw my sister and me into the bushes on the other side of the street, but we suffered only cuts and bruises. Had the bomb not landed directly in the well, it would have been a much different story! By the grace of God, we somehow made it to our farm. The doors were very thick, and the walls were made of stone, which was probably about two feet thick. Despite this, just as soon as we made it inside and closed the door, bullets from a machine gun cut it in half.

My father had caught a glimpse of us running toward town, so when he was able, he set out in the same direction searching for us. When he came to the point where the bomb hit the farmer's well, the smoke was starting to clear. A neighbor told him, "Oh! your children died! They perished because they were here when the bomb hit!" Some of the neighbors were already on their way to our farm to tell our parents they saw us killed. But thank God, He had spared us. We were alive and well although no one realized it at the time. My father continued toward the farm with bombs exploding all around him. He finally arrived and had gone no more than 50 or 60 yards inside the gate when, sure enough, a bomb dropped directly on it. The force of the explosion knocked him to the ground, and the gate was demolished, but he was uninjured. He had refused to believe we were dead. When he saw my mother, the first thing he asked her was, "Are the children okay?" She told him we were safe in our rooms. It was not until two days later that we would realize the significance of that attack. As for the cannon that had been placed so strategically, there were no pieces to be found. It had been nonsense for them to shoot the American plane because up until that time, the town had never been attacked and had not been a target. Now, three-quarters of it lay in ruin; the town was demolished. Slowly, the Germans were retreating.

A couple of days after the bombing, we saw four or five American tanks coming toward town. At first, some of the people panicked and started to run because they saw stars with five points on the tanks. They did not realize the difference between Russian stars (which were red) and American stars (which were white). Russia was not far away, and *no one* wanted to be under Russian rule. Eventually, everyone realized that these were American tanks, and they were relieved. My father and I were so excited to see the Americans that we went to the plaza to watch the convoy come into town. One of the jeeps stopped, and a soldier stepped out. He announced that all weapons were to be brought to the plaza. There was a large fountain spewing up from stones in the middle of the plaza, and this is where the weapons were to be brought. The soldiers warned that whoever was found keeping a weapon was taking a chance of being shot. We watched as the Germans surrendered their weapons. Some of them were very beautiful sabers. Another jeep carrying officers came along, and one of the officers, a Polish lieutenant, asked if anyone there spoke Polish. My father quickly spoke up, "Oh, yes. I do!" The lieutenant instructed him to take some men with him to help destroy all the weapons. He told them to hit the weapons against the stones to bend them so they could not be used. I watched the entire day as my father and the other men destroyed all the beautiful weapons.

CHAPTER FIVE

Our Father, My Father, and General Eisenhower

"For I know the plans I have for you," declares the Lord, "plans to prosper you and not to harm you, plans to give you hope and a future."

—Jer. 29:11

Moving On

After that, our boss (the old lady farmer) was even nicer to us, trying to convince us to stay at the farm. She knew we had received notice that all immigrants—Polish and other nationalities—could go to refugee camps, which were controlled by the American government. From there, the immigrants could be repatriated from camps to wherever they decided to go. The old lady offered all sorts of incentives for us to stay . . . even butter! This was a fantasy come true for my father, who had always said one day he was going to eat big chunks of butter on his bread. Up until that time, she had made his sandwiches on large chunks of week-old rye bread with a layer of butter spread so thin it barely covered the holes on the top layer. Now, she put the butter on the table and let him spread it himself, just as thick as he wanted to. She used to say, "My God, my God! What are you doing?" She also let us have all the meat we could eat. Despite all her efforts to keep us on the farm, my father eventually said, "No, we *have* to go." And go we did.

Soon, three American trucks came to town to collect any refugees who could get on the truck with their possessions to be taken to the refugee camps. We loaded our belongings and away we went! The trip to the camps took about five hours by truck. When we arrived, we found there were four camps, one of which had been an open German barracks. If you have ever seen the show, *Hogan's Heroes,* these barracks were very much like those. Here, the families were kept together with kids in bunk beds, separated only by a piece of cloth or a blanket (army-issue green blankets were plentiful). Unfortunately, the other three camps had been prison camps, and the old, barbed wire was still up and visible. Since we arrived late and the open camp was full, we were placed in one of the camps where prisoners had been kept.

An Amazing Encounter

Despite everything we went through, my father always found a way to provide for us and to better our situation. No one ever accused him of being lazy! He was a hard-working man, and he was motivated to achieve something greater for himself and his family. Somehow, he managed to get a job working in the kitchen. I thought this was great because we could get better food than everyone else in the camp (although the food they served, in general, was not too bad). But he did not stop there. He started a part-time business where he went to local farmers and bought cows, slaughtered them, and then sold the meat for cigarettes and chocolate, and so on. Cigarettes and chocolate were like gold in Germany; you could get *anything* for cigarettes and American chocolate.

One of my most vivid memories of those times was when General Eisenhower came to visit the camp, riding in a very nice convertible car. This was, of course, before he became President Eisenhower. I spent most of the time in the kitchen with my father, and this is where I was when the General came to visit. He was tasting the food and talking to the cooks, so I sneaked outside to admire his car. I was standing by the driver when my father called me to come away from it. "Don't touch that car!" he said. That is when General Eisenhower asked my father (through the translator), "Is that your son?" My father was forced to admit that I was indeed his son. "So . . ." General Eisenhower said, "He likes my car." Then he told his driver, "Go, take him for a ride!" And that is the story of how I was privileged to ride in General Eisenhower's convertible.

A Resourceful Father

> *Which of you, if your son asks for bread, will give him a stone? Or if he asks for a fish, will give him a snake? If you, then, though you are evil, know how to give good gifts to your children, how much more will your Father in heaven give good gifts to those who ask him!*
>
> —Matt. 7:9–11

After some time had passed (I do not recall how much time exactly), my father was able to have us moved to better barracks because ours were cold, and there was no privacy. At our new home, we had our own room with a little wood stove in the center, which we used for cooking and for heating the small space. Unfortunately, soon after we moved in, those barracks were deemed to be in poor condition, and they were closed. By then, my father was no longer working in the kitchen, and we had to go once a week and get provisions to cook our food. Those provisions were supplied by the American government. My father was not completely satisfied with the arrangement, so he secured a position working with the distribution of provisions. This meant we had to move again, this time to warehouses where the provisions were stored. There was only one barrack, which was shared by three families, but there were four rooms and a kitchen, and it was a comfortable enough space. My father worked loading and unloading trucks in the warehouse.

Since my father had been a butcher in the Polish Army, he was given the use of one of the Army trucks along with a driver; his new job was to go once a week to three different German towns to the butchers and collect meat to supply the refugees. I often went with him on these trips and became a regular visitor at the butcher shops. The butchers were always nice to me, and they usually had a piece of kielbasa or some other treat waiting when they saw me coming. One day I asked my father, "Dad, how come none of those kielbasas taste as good as the ones I tasted on the train when we were coming to Germany? You know, the big, long ones that looked like sausage or salami." My father laughed and said, "Well, I didn't want to tell you, but that was horse meat." I just shrugged and thought, "Well, that horse tasted really good!" As usual, my father became restless with his current position, so he began using the truck after-hours to go to farms—again to buy cows to slaughter and sell. He also gave meat to elected officials such as the police chief.

My father was able to capitalize on yet another situation while we were there. Once a week, a convoy of twelve or thirteen trucks brought supplies to our warehouse from another location. The drivers would trade vodka for gasoline, another item (like cigarettes and American chocolate) that was as good as gold. My father kept a supply of what the drivers wanted, trading for gasoline when they made their weekly run. By this time, he had built sheds where he kept pigs and chickens for our fresh eggs. He kept one of the sheds stocked with gas cans, which he would trade with the Germans for cows and other meat, eggs, and so on. Things were going well for us there and life was better than it had been in a long time.

A Sprouting Seed

> *How do you know, wife, whether you will save your husband? Or, how do you know, husband, whether you will save your wife?*
>
> —1 Cor. 7:16

If we claimed to be anything religiously, I guess we were sort of half-Catholic (if there is such a thing), and I served as an altar boy. Of course, I was the top altar boy because the priests were some of the same "officials" my father had been giving meat to. We heard about a Baptist preacher in another camp who had been having church in his quarters. My mother remembered the Baptist preacher who had told them about the Lord when they had been prisoners in Poland, so she began attending the little gatherings, but they soon encountered a problem. There were only two or three rooms and when the worshippers got together and ten to twelve started singing, not only could they be heard through the makeshift partitions, but they could be heard throughout the entire barracks! The neighbors had started to complain about the noise. At this time, my father was not going to church regularly, but he would occasionally go with my mother. He respected the preacher, so he went to the camp commander (to who he was also giving meat) and said, "Look, I need a barracks." The commander asked, "For what?" So, my father replies, "I want to open a church for those people." The commander was Catholic and there was some hesitation, but since my father did so many favors for him, he agreed. Our barracks consisted of four rooms, which were shared with only one other family. Once he moved the family out and moved some of the walls, we had a Baptist church in our building. I am not exactly sure when my father came to know Christ (I would estimate somewhere around 1947), but after that he attended every service and that is how we became Baptists.

When the priest found out we were attending a Baptist church, he no longer wanted me to serve as an altar boy. That was fine with me because, to be honest, my troubles as an altar boy had started even earlier. The other altar boys had become jealous because I had more privileges with the priest—ironically, because of my father. They forced me to look in the golden chalice, which was forbidden. When they told the priest what I had done, he suspended me from my duties for a week. I am not sure which action weighed more heavily into his decision—my becoming a Baptist or my looking into the golden chalice, but either way, after that point, the priest decided I was no longer fit for service, and I was excommunicated.

CHAPTER SIX

The Long Journey Begins

Be joyful in hope, patient in affliction, faithful in prayer.

—Rom. 12:12

A Change of Plans

Our goal was to come to the United States. Occasionally, we would hear announcements through the walls in the office that a trip had opened up to Canada or the United States, or other countries. Three times we heard of the opportunity to come to the United States, three times we filled out paperwork, and signed up to go through the process of getting clearance by the doctors, and so on, and three times the trip was canceled.

Rumors started to spread about the fate of the camp, including rumors that it might be given to the Russians. This caused folks to be a little bit on edge, including my father. When we heard of a possible trip to Brazil, we planned to take it. Before we were to leave for Brazil, however, an opportunity came for us to go to Canada. The deal was this: A certain number of families were needed to go and start a town at a certain location. They would be placed in the middle of nowhere by a lake, but they would be supplied with all the wood they needed to get started. They would also be provided with tools to cut and build as well as firearms to hunt with. My father signed on for that right away but, unfortunately, they were unable to get enough families to commit to the deal, and it had to be canceled too. He decided we would go to Brazil and then on to America from there. Finally, the trip to Brazil went through, and we were on our way.

We were taken first from Germany to Italy, and there we waited for the ship that was to take us to our destination in Brazil. While in Italy, we stayed in a camp that had once been used as an army camp with—you guessed it—barracks. This time, the ladies were in one barracks and the men in another. We waited here for eight months for a ship to take us to Brazil. I am not sure of the exact location of this camp, but I do know it was located close to the volcanic mountain, Vesuvius. I remember watching fire shoot up from the volcano at night. Sometimes, at night when it was quiet, we could hear gurgling sounds coming from the direction of the mountain.

This camp was very memorable to me because there, I had my first experience eating oranges. A twelve-foot cement wall surrounded the camp, and we could not go out of it. Occasionally, a few adults would be taken on a small bus into the city, and guards would go along for protection; however, children were never allowed to go on these excursions. I was fascinated with the doorway at one side of the camp where a man stood selling oranges. Some people had money to buy oranges, but others traded clothes and other belongings for them. I was so crazy about the oranges that one day I made the mistake of trading my shoes for them, a decision my parents made sure I lived to regret! There was a plantation of orange groves on the other side of the compound wall and of course, I was fascinated with it. It was so large that I could not see the end of the rows! I had two little friends who were also refugees from Germany, and we loved to play around the camp and get into mischief. One day, we discovered a pile of wood stacked against a wall near the kitchen. The wood in this stack was intended to be used for firewood to cook our food, but it was also the perfect place for three little boys to play and hide in. It was only a matter of time before we discovered at the bottom of the stack was a drainage hole leading out of the compound. The hole had been completely covered with wood, so we began to dig deeper and deeper until it was large enough for us to crawl out under the wall. We started sneaking out into the grove and stealing oranges at night. We were not being good boys, but that is what we did and that is how we had a steady supply of oranges.

We spent several months in Italy waiting for the ship to take us to Brazil. Only two days before we were to leave, we received news that we would be boarding an American troupe carrier named *The General McRae*. This ship was so old that the US Army no longer used it for fighting, but it had been repurposed to transport refugees from one country to another. We packed everything we had unpacked, and we were ready to go. It was so early that the sun had not yet risen when two trucks came into the compound, and we were loaded onto one, our luggage onto another. The journey from the compound took about one hour before we arrived at the port in Naples.

Tossed by the Sea (All Expenses Paid)

> *When you pass through the waters, I will be with you; and when you pass through the rivers, they will not sweep over you.*
>
> —Isa. 43:2a

The first day on *The General McRae* was great! Within a couple of hours of boarding, everyone was settled in. The ladies were on one part of the ship and the men on another. The beds were stacked army bunks—some two and some three tall. Two of my friends and I took a three-bed bunk close to the bathroom, and I was on the top. The ship started moving out of the port and the announcement came for supper time. We excitedly jumped out of bed and headed to the dining hall. Each person was given a large metal tray, and each person made their way down a huge buffet-style serving line. We were served as much as we wanted and, oh, this was great! We all ate good and plenty. However, during the night as we traveled further out of the port and into the open sea, things started to become a little shaky. The next morning at breakfast, I noticed there were not as many people as there had been for supper the night before, but that did not stop *me* from enjoying it . . . it was great!

On the second day, the ship began to shake violently from one side to the other as the waves grew larger and larger. By nightfall and supper time, there was almost no one in the cafeteria because most of the passengers were sick. My father and I went to the cafeteria and ate because there was good fried fish on the menu. The shaking worsened during the night to the point that we could hardly stay in our beds. The next morning when we went to breakfast, my father and I were the only ones in the cafeteria! During the day the waves became even larger and I remember thinking that it was almost as if the sea was heavy. I went up on deck and saw the front of the ship going up, up, up . . . it looked like it was going to hit the sky! Then just as sure as it went up, it came right back down until I thought it was going head-first into the water! This continued all day, but we had to watch the storm through the windows because we were not allowed to go out onto the porches. The next morning everyone was allowed back on deck. I was amazed to find dead fish scattered all over the place, right where the waves had left them. Someone finally decided to check on our luggage and found the large trunks had been completely turned over in the storage room and slid to the opposite side from where they had been placed.

The wind began to slow, the waters became calm, and by late evening the air had become warm. My friends and I decided to lay down in the corridor leading to the bathroom. This was because the corridor was cooler than our room as it was adjacent to an outside wall that was underwater. We were lying on blankets in the corridor in the middle of the night when we were suddenly awakened by flooding water! We quickly found ourselves covered with seawater, so we ran outside as fast as we could to find help. We found a sailor, but he could not speak English, and we were unable to explain to him what was happening, so we decided to show him. We led him to the corridor where the water was continuing to rise. He immediately locked the compartment, and we were told to remain on deck for the remainder of the night. The ship was so old that a hole had opened up in the wall, and seawater was leaking into the corridor where we had been sleeping. Of all the places on the ship, what were the chances of the leak happening near us? Once dawn broke, the crew began to repair the ship by welding a metal plate to the damaged side, and we were eventually allowed to return to our quarters.

The rest of the day was uneventful, and the atmosphere was comfortable. At least for us, it was. Many of the passengers were still sick, especially the ladies. Every morning, noontime, and evening very few people came to the cafeteria. My father and I never missed one single meal because we could not believe the quality of the food, not to mention the fact that we could have all we wanted!

On Sunday, a Catholic priest asked permission to perform a mass and then asked if anyone on the ship had served as an altar boy. One of my friends volunteered for me, telling the priest that I used to be an altar boy. When the priest came to me and asked me to perform the mass I said, "Oh yes, I would be happy to, but the only problem is that I am not Catholic anymore." He looked surprised and asked, "Well, what are you then?" I explained to him that my parents were Baptist, so I was a Baptist now. He decided he did not care about that. He said, "If you remember how to do the mass to help me, I'd be glad to use you." Of course, I remembered all the prayers in Latin and all that was required to perform the traditions, so the following Sunday I served as an altar boy for the mass.

A few days later, we crossed the equatorial line. A big feast was prepared, and there was a celebration for those who were crossing the line for the first time, including a couple of the sailors. The celebration was unbelievable! There were many fun activities on the ship that day. No one was told what to expect, and each person was voluntarily blindfolded and led to a different area or activity. For example, a large tube was set next to a pool of water and used as a slide. To make the slide even better, the inside of the tube was coated with oil! Some of the younger ladies thought it might be fun and decided to participate, but they regretted it when all was said and done. They really *did not* look so good once they were dipped in oil and water. Boy, did they ever have a time trying to wash the oil out of their hair!

On the following day, the weather was fair and some of the ladies decided to go on deck. Chairs were brought out because most of the passengers had been sick below and wanted to get some fresh air. However, by late afternoon the boat started to shake again. Some of the passengers decided to stay on deck and again, some of the passengers became sick. Everyone was told to go back inside, except for the ones who had not become sick; they were told to stay to help clean up behind the others. My father was elected to help, so naturally, I stayed to help alongside him. When I was finished, I went down to our quarters to find one of my friends had decided to lay down on my top bunk. No sooner had we started a conversation than he leaned over the bed and vomited all over me. That was the closest I came to being sick for the entire trip, but I immediately went topside and the nausea passed. There were approximately two hundred immigrants on the ship, and I believe my father and I were the only two who did not get sick.

No more than a couple of days after that, we woke up to find the ship had slowed. We went outside to see what had happened and found we had docked a small distance outside the harbor. The trip from Naples to Rio de Janeiro had taken fourteen days. An announcement was made that we would disembark there to be taken to shore. A small boat came alongside the ship, and families were taken ashore little by little as the boat returned for the next group. When it was finally our turn, we boarded the boat and a few minutes later, we were on the island.

CHAPTER SEVEN

A New Land

Cheerfully share your home with those who need a meal or a place to stay.

—1 Pet. 4:9 (NLT)

The Church's Role

Isla de Flores means the Isle of Flowers. One could certainly see how the island had been named because of the varieties and plentiful amounts of beautiful flowers found there. This island was so close to the mainland that if you stood at one point on the end of the island, you could see the streets of Rio. In fact, you could almost see what was displayed in the store windows. The water separating the island from the mainland was very deep during high tide, but on some days, when the tide went out and the water was about knee-deep, one could easily cross the divide.

Each family was given 50 cruzeiro, which at that time was worth no more than about 40 cents. We were once again housed in Army barracks—again, with men in one and women in another. At supper time we went to the kitchen where we were given metal plates with dividers like those we used on the ship. We were served beans and rice, a small piece of meat, a half piece of toast, a banana, and freshly baked bread. I loved the bananas, especially when I put them inside the fresh bread along with the meat, and each day this is what I ate. Our people typically did not care for beans and rice; they preferred bacon. As it turns out, the more fat on bacon, the cheaper it was by the pound, so they purchased it by the pound and brought it onto the island. They quickly learned that fatty meat does not last long in the South American heat, and on one occasion a doctor had to be called to the island because everyone had become sick from eating spoiled bacon.

After a few days, we were called to the office to determine whether it was our "time" to depart for Brazil. We were asked if we knew anyone in Brazil. My father told them he wanted to go to the church in Sao Paulo because he knew some of the elders there. They told us to get ready because the next day, we would go to the train station to be taken to Sao Paulo. The next morning came, and about twenty families were loaded on the boat and taken to the train station on the mainland. We were all placed into one car, the one at the end of the train (that sounds familiar). I sat by the window as we waited. The locals tried to talk to us, but we did not know the language and could not understand them. I will always remember a kind lady who brought a big container of popcorn and gave it to my sister and me. That was great! Eventually, the train slowly began to move, and we were on our way. We traveled through the night until we arrived at another station.

The next morning, we noticed our wagon had been disconnected, but the rest of the train had gone on ahead! A small locomotive hooked to our wagon and, very slowly, began to move. We traveled about ten to twenty minutes before we pulled off the main tracks at a big warehouse. There were stairs with rails that led to the entrance of the building, and the entrance was about four feet wide. As soon as we entered the building, we saw we were not the only family there. Each family was assigned a small cubicle with bunk beds and although the cubicles were built on a wooden platform, there was no roof! Because of this, the mosquitos feasted on us. The morning came, and we were back to eating rice and beans, bananas, bread, and a little piece of meat. We were glad when the pastor from the church was notified, and two days later he came to get us. He agreed we could stay at the church until we had jobs and a place to live. We quickly prepared to leave the warehouse, knowing we had yet to walk for approximately a half-hour to the station, and the train was scheduled to leave in two hours. We finally arrived at the station, boarded the train, and departed for Sao Paulo. The trip took about two hours but once we arrived, we still had to walk for another thirty minutes before we reached the church. We were very relieved when two men came to meet us and helped us drag our luggage the rest of the way.

When we finally arrived at the church, we were given one room with four single beds in the basement. The beds were nice and clean and comfortable. We stayed at the church for about three weeks while my father looked for a job. He was skilled in plumbing and other handiwork, so in the meantime, he did repairs at the church. The church continued to feed and care for us until my father eventually found a job bottling milk in a milk house. He worked the night shift and did not make much money, but he had been allowed to bring home a liter of milk to his family after each shift he worked, and this was helpful.

Venturing Out

> *And my God will meet all your needs according to the riches of his glory in Christ Jesus.*
>
> —Phil. 4:19

After about a month and a half of staying at the church, we decided to look for a house of our own where we could pay rent. We discovered it was impossible to buy or rent a house in the center of the city with our income, so my father decided to look for a place to live outside of town in the villages. We visited a Baptist church we had heard about in the villages, and the pastor was able to help us to find a house. It was owned by one of the church members, and it consisted of two small rooms with a little kitchen in the back of the house. Another family lived there too, with a little boy who was a little younger than me. Even though living in this area made for a good one-hour trip each evening to where my father worked, it was the best we could do, and we got by.

School had not yet started, so at night my father sometimes took me to the factory where he worked. There was a typical tall factory chimney, which I usually slept near to keep warm. The factory was fenced with a high wall, and I soon discovered a hole in the wall where repairs had been made but never finished. My father would occasionally bring an extra empty two-liter container, which he would fill during the night and bring to me. Just before his shift ended, I would go to the outside hallway to wait for him, unnoticed. Whatever we could get, we would sell to buy butter because, for many, many days, we could not afford butter and had to eat dry bread. Each day we ate the same thing . . . rice and beans. Sometimes, we had a little piece of meat, and sometimes we did not. My mother started to work a little bit, and we lived this way for many months, but we were able to pay rent and survive.

It was not long before I discovered I had a problem of my own. The daughter of the owner of the house we rented began to viciously pick on me. Her nickname for me was *bicho de agua*, which is loosely translated to "*monster from the sea*" (because we came over the seas to Brazil). We had been frequently called this while in Brazil, and it infuriated me, so I soon came up with a plan to get her back, but I would have to wait until the right time. You see, it was my responsibility to cook the beans while my parents were at work. The beans had to cook for a long time and had to be watched constantly; otherwise, the water cooked out, and the beans dried and burned very easily. This happened to me a lot. When my parents came home, the beans were burned and their response was, "You will get it for that because you don't pay attention!" To make matters worse, sometimes the owner's daughter would sneak around and extinguish the fire under the beans using a glass of water. The fire was generated by charcoal in a small metal box with small legs and ignited by a little liquid. When she threw the water on the fire, I had to restart it and begin cooking all over again!

One day, as I was fanning the fire and moving the charcoals, I let the metal stick get good and hot. This time, when she came to throw water on the fire, I took the red-hot metal stick and swung it at her to keep her from coming close. Sure enough, she was branded! The stick had left a noticeable red line on her flesh. For some reason, this created a problem, and we were forced to move out. Again, we could not find an affordable house, so we rented half a house with another family. Like us, this family had come from Germany, and they had two boys, so there were a total of eight people living in a two-room house with a kitchen built off to the side. It was very awkward because to get outside, we had to walk through their room. It was inconvenient, but we were living.

Bullies

> *Though I walk in the midst of trouble, you preserve my life. You stretch out your hand against the anger of my foes; with your right hand you save me.*
>
> —Ps. 138:7

Summer passed, and it was time for school to start. I could not speak the language, so one of our friends from church who had been in Brazil for a time took me to school to register. As it turned out, the language barrier was not the only problem I had to face once schooltime came. The children picked on me terribly, calling me a monster and more. Sometimes, I took it patiently, but there were other times I could not take it and fought back, so I stayed in trouble for fighting. Because school was held at different times, I was able to sneak in without being seen. Unfortunately, we all left to go home at the same time, and this is when a boy who lived near the school started to pick on me. He was always with his gang (he was the leader), so I had to tolerate his punching and kicking for many months. One day after school, I found him walking home alone, so I stayed back some distance, hoping he did not see me. As it turned out, I was not the only student who did not like him because it was not long before a group of about five boys jumped him and started beating him up. Thinking about it now, I am not sure whether I was being stupid or brave, but I came to his defense, and we both got our share. After the boys left, the gang leader looked at me and asked, "Why did you help me?" I responded by telling him, "I really do not know." From that time on I was respected, and no one could touch me or call me names because I had the respect of the gang who would come to my defense.

We had to move again. My father had found a better-paying job working with a plumbing company that contracted to repair old houses and install sewers. We found a house on the north side of Sao Paulo, an entire house we would have to ourselves! I was transferred to another school in a new village, and my problems started again, the same as before.

One day I found a stainless-steel cable that was about one meter long. I tied a loop in one end and asked my father to weld a little lead ball in the other end. When he asked me what it was for, I was very vague in my explanation and just told him I needed it. He did not ask any more questions but went ahead and made it for me. I used it to protect myself by swinging the cable over my head in a circle, and the kids could not even get close to me. That is how I got by until school was out. Before school started again, my father informed me that he had found yet another house, this time on the south side of Sao Paulo. Travel to Sao Paulo took about an hour by bus from our current house, but at the new house, it would take about an hour and twenty minutes, by train. Work on the house was delayed, however, so we did not move in right away.

"Working" Toward a Future Calling

> *For we are God's handiwork, created in Christ Jesus to do good works, which God prepared in advance for us to do.*
>
> —Eph. 2:10

I finally reached my fourteenth birthday. This was an important milestone because, in Brazil, I could go to work at the age of fourteen. I received my document for working which looked like a passport booklet with a picture, along with my name and general information. I would be required to submit this document to anyone who employed me, and upon termination, I was to get it back. My father's friend worked about two blocks from the office where these booklets were issued. His job was to take pictures for the documents, and I was hired as his photographer. The work was not difficult, but I hated it because I had to get up at four o'clock in the morning to take the bus ride for about an hour or so, and then I had to walk about twenty more minutes before I finally got to work. I had to be at work before the office opened at six o'clock. This was challenging for me as a teenager . . . especially when I stayed overnight with friends and had a difficult time waking up the next morning.

It just so happened that an optician worked next to the photography shop . . . I had no idea how significant this would prove to be. The owner of the optical shop would come and visit with us when he had no customers. My photography job ended at noon every day, and as I was leaving the shop after work one day, the optician approached me and asked, "Do you go home this early every day?" I told him that I did, so he asked, "Would you like to make a couple of cruzeiros?" I said, "Sure. What do I have to do?" He explained that all I would have to do is pick up some merchandise and deliver it to him. In Brazil, an optician could order lenses or frames over the phone, but they were required to pick up the merchandise themselves.

For about two weeks, I would finish my first job at noon, and then I would go pick up merchandise for the optician. One day the optician asked, "How much do you make over there?" I told him I made five hundred cruzeiros per month. Then he asked me if I would like to come to work for him. He told me I would be working from nine o'clock a.m. to six o'clock p.m. I could take two hours for lunch, and the pay was one thousand cruzeiros. Boy, that hit me like a ton of bricks! I wanted it! My only fear was that my father would be angry with me for quitting his friend. I asked the optician to give me until the next day for an answer, and he agreed. I went home and told my father about the job offer and, just like I thought, he was not too happy about it. He said, "My friend needs you to be there because he leaves early." I thought to myself, yeah, because I am running the photography shop, so he can come and go for an hour or so, come back and get some money, and then go again! I thought about it and said to my father, "No, I'm taking the job." I told him that I could not stand getting up so early in the morning and I was going to quit the photography shop. I do not have to tell you that my father did not like it.

The following day was a Wednesday. I worked for the photographer until nine o'clock and then I told him I needed to go talk to the optician. When he asked why I just told him I had to talk to him about something. I asked the optician when I could start. He said, "It's up to you. You can start tomorrow or wait until Monday." I was not sure yet, so I told him I would let him know by the end of the day. I went back to my father's friend and told him I was quitting and was going to work for the optician because I could not keep the hours his job required. Oh, was he ever angry! He threatened to talk to my parents until I told him, "That's okay, I already talked to them." He became even angrier; then I grew angry and even angrier, until eventually, I said, "That's it! I'm leaving today!" Sure enough, God saw fit that I would work for the optician for eight years and learn the trade before we were to leave for the United States.

We finally moved into our new house in the town of Carapicuiba. It was a small brick house with only one room (which we all slept in) and a wooden kitchen outside. My father announced we would build another room so I could have my own. I was enjoying the hours on my new job with the optician, which consisted of picking up materials and cleaning the shop. After a month or two he says to me, "Would you like to learn to be an optician?" I was so excited I said, "Sure I would!" He instructed me to sweep the shop and wash the sidewalk when I arrived in the mornings, and afterward not to do any cleaning but to just watch what he did and work with him. "I will teach you to be an optician," he said. That sounded wonderful to me, mostly because I was embarrassed for other young people to see me out cleaning the sidewalks. I had already met a couple of young people in the Baptist church nearby us, and they took the same train as I did to come to work in the mornings. Some of them arrived fifteen minutes later, so they would see me cleaning the sidewalks, which I found to be a little bit humiliating.

Eventually, my father learned the code requirements and decided to quit his job to begin contracting on his own. He took on four or five houses at a time, doing plumbing and sewers. I only worked until noon on Saturday, so I went wherever he was working and helped him until evening. Sometimes, I had to dig sewage. Because the houses were made of brick, I sometimes had to dig a line in the wall to put in pipes. I was helping, but it was not easy work. We were finally making some money and were able to pay off the little bit we had borrowed to buy the house. It was in a new area; I had a new job, we attended a new church, and everything was going well, so we decided to build an addition to our house. We built a kitchen and extra room for me and while we were at it, we decided to build a good-sized storage room. By the time we finished the renovations, we decided to finish out the storage area as one nice, big room. It was not like any of the rooms we ever had before. During this time, the electric company brought power to the area for the first time. This was a great thing for many reasons, but first of all, we were able to take hot water showers. We were also able to buy appliances such as a refrigerator, so we could keep meat for many days, unlike before when we had to buy it every day.

> *The greatest among you should be like the youngest,*
> *and the one who rules like the one who serves.*
>
> —Luke 22:26b

Things were going well. We became active in a small Baptist church where most of the members were young people. With time, I made many friends—boys and girls—and everyone seemed to like me. The end of the year came and to my surprise, I was appointed Youth Leader. Because we had no cars or other recreation, the large room that had been built for storage became a place for the young people to gather and play games and sing the songs we had learned at church. It was a good time of fellowship.

CHAPTER EIGHT

"Hunting" for Excitement!

Then God said, "Let us make mankind in our image, in our likeness, so that they may rule over the fish in the sea and the birds in the sky, over the livestock and all the wild animals, and over all the creatures that move along the ground.

—Gen. 1:26

Creatures in the Night

Time passed and my boss at the optical shop began to take frequent trips, hunting, and fishing expeditions. I showed a strong interest in these trips and each time he returned, I asked him many, many questions. One day he said, "Look, we are going hunting in a couple of weeks; I will see if we can make arrangements for my brother to stay in the shop for about two weeks, and I will take you with me." Oh, I was so happy about this! Just like he said he would do, he arranged for his brother to watch the shop, and I had the chance to go with him on my first fishing and hunting expedition.

The first day of the expedition finally came, and it was mostly spent traveling by train. Then we were met by others from the expedition with two trucks loaded down with equipment. We rode for most of the next day, sitting on the equipment for the entire ride. The ride took us through dense jungles; deserted areas; and wide, open plains before we finally reached the river at nightfall. There, a large barge was waiting for us, and we loaded the equipment we had been riding on all day onto the barge. We went downriver for a couple of hours before stopping at an Indian village. Jose, our guide, joined us there. I found it very interesting that the custom of this tribe was to stretch their bottom lips with a plate (along with some other customs which were very strange to me). We stayed for a couple of hours in the village before we resumed our journey down the river.

We traveled downriver for another day before finally stopping at a building on the corner of a tributary. It was basically a mud building covered with bamboo sticks, with a couple of windows and doors on each end. Because it was so long and narrow, our sleeping arrangements consisted of hammocks strung from one wall to the other. This allowed us to sleep off the ground to hopefully avoid some of the creatures that crawled around there at night.

When we arrived on the first night, it was late; everyone was tired, and everyone fell asleep right away. Everyone except me, that is. I was very tired but could not bring myself to sleep because of the night noises. There were constant bird sounds and other unknown noisy animal creature sounds, so the next night I decided to sleep on the barge. The barge was docked a small distance off the land because the water's edge was not deep enough for it to come near. This meant we had to use a small boat to shuttle back and forth from the bank to the barge. As it turned out, this idea for sleeping arrangements was not a very good one either. There were many crocodiles in this river and apparently, crocodiles cannot focus or see very well in the dark because they kept running into the barge. These were large crocodiles and when they hit the barge it shook. Once again, I was up all night. I eventually gave up and decided to go back and sleep in the hammocks with everyone else. This time I set my hammock close to the Indian guide stationed near the door at one end of the building. Unfortunately, the jungle noises had not gotten any quieter.

It was a clear night, and the stars lit up the sky so much that it was brighter *outside* the building than it was *inside* it. Although the building was long and narrow, more than 30 men were sleeping in hammocks with one hammock strung close to the next. The noises inside the building were not always pleasant, either. After a while, I heard a *new* noise, unlike the ones I had heard before. This one seemed to be coming from the door at the opposite end of the building. I kept listening and trying to identify the noise as it came closer and closer until it seemed to be directly over my head. We each had a flashlight, and because I wanted to know what was making the noise, I shined my light on the ceiling above me, and then I froze. Sure enough, a *really, really, really BIG* snake was on the rafter directly above me. I should explain that we slept fully clothed and armed with .45 mm automatic handguns supplied by my boss's father-in-law. (He was a major in the army and supplied rifles and handguns for the expedition.) In addition to the .45 on my side, a rifle was standing against the wall. I wanted to reach for my .45, but I was so terrified I could not even move my flashlight! This thing's head had already passed by me, and its tail was still on the other end of the building! Eventually, I regained my sense and called for the guide. He was sleeping right next to me, snoring like a locomotive, but I was finally able to wake him up. "Jose! Look what's up there in the ceiling," I said as the snake was sliding in between the rafters. Jose looked up and said, "Oh, don't worry; she's just looking for the birds." I thought to myself, well I hope she does not confuse me with the birds! The snake crept slowly through the rafters until it reached the end of the building and was gone. So again, I could not sleep for fear that the snake might come back if she could not find any birds! Jose, of course, just turned over on his other side and never stopped snoring.

Unbelievable!

The next day came, and we went exploring for food supplies, and then we decided to go hunt for wild pigs. We were walking in single file behind Jose when suddenly he jumped and came to a dead stop. I was wondering what had happened when I noticed that on his gaucho pants (which were tucked into his boots) was hanging something that looked like a lizard. If it was a lizard, it was at least a 3-foot-long lizard. I watched him, thinking to myself, *"What is he going to do now?"* I watched as Jose calmly took a knife from his belt and severed the creature from its head. The body fell but the head was still attached to his pants.

Jose resumed walking just like nothing had happened, and everyone followed behind in single file. Eventually, we came to a clearing where we stopped, and I had to ask, "Jose, why doesn't the head fall off? Isn't it dead"? He said to me, "Well, that head won't open its mouth until sundown." I thought . . . *"All right, he is pulling my leg now."* I knew that they always played jokes on the new ones, so I did not believe him. I watched him closely for the rest of the day. We shot two pigs and brought them back to the camp at the end of the day and, still, the lizard head was with us. Jose said to me, "Ok, watch what happens when the sun goes down." He did not need to tell me because I was constantly keeping an eye on him. We were sitting around the campfire when the last rays of the sun dipped behind the hill. Suddenly, the head opened its mouth and fell to the ground. I could not believe my eyes! I asked him why this was, and if it was dangerous. He said, "Yes, it is very poisonous and once it clamps onto its victim it cannot open its mouth; it keeps pumping venom into whatever it bites. It's usually fatal." That would explain why he seemed to be more than a little bit alarmed when he was not sure whether it had bitten into more than his pants! This was one of the more interesting experiences on the trip, and after that one, I decided to stay in the camp. I helped the cook or did whatever I could so that I did not have to go back on the hunts.

Fortunately, most of the days were spent fishing. We caught fish, dried them with salt, and then put them in barrels to take home. However, they decided to go on another hunting expedition and by early afternoon, they had brought home four wild pigs. Suddenly, we heard unusual noises coming from the river and noticed the birds were mysteriously flying away. I had noticed the crocodiles often came out of the water to bask in the sun, and I had also noticed some of the crocodiles' tails were missing except for the bones. I had never bothered to ask why. This time I saw the crocodiles *running* out of the water onto the bank. I asked one of the men, "What's happening?" and he told me, "The piranhas are coming." Oh well, *that* explained it. I was one of at least ten or eleven men who were on their first expedition, so the more experienced hunters decided to demonstrate to us just how powerful these fish were. They tied one pig's legs together with a rope and hung the pig on a tree branch, which extended out over the water. It was not long before we heard a noise rising from the water, and the water began to boil. Slowly, they lowered the pig into the water by its feet. I remember thinking it looked like French fries being lowered into boiling oil. Within a couple of minutes, there was nothing left of the pig except bones. I could not believe I had been washing my hands and face in that river, and I decided right then and there that would not be happening again.

Another interesting event on this expedition happened on the trip home when we turned a corner, and a high hill came into view. This hill was covered with dense vegetation except for one area that was completely cleared; not even a blade of grass or a stick was to be found there. The clear area was approximately one-quarter mile wide, but it continued over the hill, so we could not see how far it went. When I asked why this was, I was told it was the result of soldier ants passing through. They explained to me that when the ants pass through, they devour anything green. It was fascinating to know that tiny ants could do so much damage. The trip lasted two weeks, but to me, it felt like two months. After only a couple of experiences, it had become an uncomfortable place to be.

CHAPTER NINE

The Day My Life Changed

And be sure your sin will find you out.

—Num. 32:23b (KJV)

Looking for a Pretty Girl, Finding Jesus (aka "The Pink Shirt Story")

Three weeks after we returned home, a baptism was held at our church. I did not totally understand it, but I chose to be baptized because some of my friends were being baptized. (This was only a couple of months before I was elected to the position of youth leader.) I could handle most aspects of this position with no problem except for the preaching and all that went along with it. I was never good at speaking, and I never will be. I had a guidebook of "How-To" for youth services, so time went by and everything was going fine.

We heard there was going to be a big crusade in San Paulo, which is about twenty-five kilometers from where we lived. A Pentecostal healing evangelist was scheduled to come, and it was mostly Pentecostal churches that had been invited to participate. I decided I would go to the event, along with two of my friends. We agreed not to let anyone know we were going because, at that time, Baptists and Pentecostals did not mix. We decided to go mostly because many, many churches would be represented, which meant there would be many, many girls. It was to take place at a large theatre or convention hall, which was made of aluminum and shaped like a dome, seating about 5,000 people.

We arrived at the arena approximately one hour before the service started, but when we walked in, we could only find a place to stand halfway up the middle aisle; everything else was full. About twenty minutes after we arrived, the doors were closed behind us because the room was full of people. There was no air conditioning in the building, and the air was not circulating very well because there were only a couple of windows on the side, two doors in the front, and two doors in the back. We were miserable, but we had come on a mission.

The music started while we were playing around (trying to get attention from the girls), and after a couple of songs were sung, a little man took the stage. He was probably no more than five feet two or five feet three. He said, "We'll have a short reading of the Bible, and then we're going to have a healing service." Well, this was all fine because we—at least I—did not care much about whatever he was going to do. I was doing what I came to do, which was looking at the girls. He preached for approximately ten to fifteen minutes. Do not ask me what he said or the title of his sermon, because the only thing I remembered during the sermon was how very, very hot it was in the arena. As a matter of fact, during the sermon, a lady passed out. Because she was on a side aisle, she had to be passed overhead from one person to another to get her to the door.

Eventually, the preacher said, "Now we're going to have a healing service." He walked down from the platform to the front, which had been packed with additional seating and people on crutches or in wheelchairs. A large man stood in front of me and blocked my direct view from what was going on at the front, but that was okay by me; they were doing their thing, and we were doing ours. The evangelist began praying and people started clapping and "hallelujah-ing" all over the arena because apparently someone laid his crutches down and started to walk. Next, a man in a wheelchair was brought before the evangelist. I could not see his feet, but I could see that his hands were twisted. The evangelist began to explain that the man had a disease that had crippled his hands and feet, and he had been this way for many, many years. This one caught my attention because I could see him a little better than the others. The evangelist said to the audience, "Everyone, pray and this man will be healed!" As he placed his hand over the man's head, I wondered to myself how much the evangelist had paid the man to perform. The evangelist started to speak and then stopped suddenly. He said nothing, but he just looked around the arena and everything got quiet.

I was very hot and had been sweating but when he stopped praying and started looking around, I started to feel a cold sweat. It was conviction, and I could feel a connection between him and me. He took his hands off the crippled man's head and then he said, "There is someone here who feels all this has been premeditated or pre-fixed" (maybe not exactly these words because he was speaking Portuguese, but with the same meaning). When he said that, I started to sweat. At that point, I started looking back to find a way out, but there was none. The building was full of people, the doors were locked, and there was no way out. It was the first time I had experienced anything like that because we had not seen stuff like this in the Baptist churches. I could see there were other people in the same boat as I was, doubting. He asked for the person who did not believe the healing was genuine to raise their hand. As doubters began to raise their hands, he said, "No, not you. No, not you." Probably ten times he repeated, "No, not you." With every moment that passed, I became more and more scared. I was very shy at that time, and I was in an arena with 5,000 people. But the thing that affected me most was the realization that I was playing around with the power of God Almighty, and this really scared me. At that moment I was so struck with the reality that I just hoped the floor would open up and swallow me. I wanted to be *anywhere* but there. I watched the evangelist as he went running back up onto the high platform, turned, and pointed. "It's in this section right here, right in the middle." Well, that did it because he was practically pointing right at me. Someone directly behind me raised their hand, but the evangelist said, "No, not you," and every time this would happen, people would turn around to see who had raised their hand. The gentleman in front of me shifted to turn around to look behind him and suddenly I was uncovered, exposed . . . I could no longer hide. Sure enough, the evangelist immediately shouted, "Yes! You there with the pink shirt . . . you! Come here!" Oh boy! I looked back again to make sure there was no way out, and there was none. There was no one behind me in a hot pink shirt, either.

I started to come up with a plan. I figured I would go toward the front and as soon as I got there, I would hit one of the side doors and make my escape. People were "helping" me because the rows were tiered, the seats had armrests, and I had to walk on the armrests to get to the front. Once I reached the last armrest, the evangelist was waiting for me and grabbed me by the arm. I tried to get away from him, but he would not let go. He took me to the crippled man in the wheelchair and said, "Look at his hands, look at his feet. . . . Can God heal someone like this?" At that moment I did not answer because all that was on my mind was getting out of there! He was holding my arm very tightly and then he said, "I'm going to pray for this man. God's people are going to help me pray, and God is going to heal him." I remember him asking, "Do you believe?" I have no idea what I answered. He prayed a short prayer (all his prayers were short). During the prayer, I watched the man as his feet started to shake . . . then slowly and little by little, they began to straighten. Then, I watched as his hands gradually became straighter until they looked normal.

I cannot explain what I felt, but it seemed like I might die from fear because it was as if I was standing before God Almighty, defiling His love and kindness toward me. I understood that I was face to face with a power that was beyond my comprehension. The evangelist said to two men on either side of the crippled man, "Stand him up." They helped the man to stand and, very slowly, he started to take a step forward and then another and then another until he stood alone. It was like a nightmare for me; it seemed like I had died and was watching all this happening outside of myself. The people started to praise God, singing Hallelujah and Glory to God, and it was like I was not really there. I do not remember much about what happened after that. I am not sure whether I passed out or what exactly happened, but when I came to myself, I was behind the curtains on the platform and people were praying for me. Slowly I realized what had happened, and I understood *that* was the time God touched me.

Denominations and Dogma

> *You were taught, with regard to your former way of life, to put off your old self, which is being corrupted by its deceitful desires; to be made new in the attitude of your minds.*
>
> —Eph. 4:22–23

My life changed drastically after this encounter with God. I started to search the Scriptures and was hungry to know more about God and his glory and to walk closer with Him. On the way home from our church, we passed by a Pentecostal church. Although our church frowned on attending Pentecostal churches, I visited a couple of times. I also began asking my pastor some questions about the Holy Spirit and the baptism in the Holy Spirit, and what the Scripture had to say about it. He was not happy to have these conversations. In fact, I was soon called into a board meeting where I was rebuked and told not to do this again, so we only visited that church during special occasions or holiday services.

Eventually, the youth asked me why we never went back. I had to explain to them that the pastor had told me not to do it anymore. At that point, they asked me whether I would be willing to go with them if *they* organized a visit. I encouraged them to make a list and have everyone who wanted to go sign up, and I would sign and go along with them. So, we went to a picnic with the people from the Pentecostal church and had a good time. Sure enough, when we went to our church the following Sunday, it was announced that I was "invited" to a board meeting on Monday night. The time came for the meeting and as I expected, the pastor reminded me, "I told you not to do it, but you disobeyed us." I tried to defend myself and explained I only went with everyone else and that they had asked to go. He told me he was aware everyone signed a list, but that I was responsible. He explained that instead of telling them not to go, I went along with them. Well, that was the end of the line for me at that church, and I was kicked out.

On the evening of the board meeting, as I left the church approximately forty to forty-five young people were waiting to see what had happened, so I told them. "I am not supposed to show my face anymore in this church because of what I did, disobeying the pastor's orders." A few of the youth came to me and said, "What are we going to do?" I told them they probably should not do anything because their parents were in the church. I did not want them to pay the same price I had. Some of them would not accept this and wanted to know where I planned to go to church now that I had been kicked out. I told them, "Well, I went last Sunday to such-and-such church" because I had already started looking for myself. However, there were certain things at this church that I did not agree with or want to be a part of. Gradually, more and more young people started going with me every Sunday to different churches to see if we could find one that we were comfortable with, but we could not seem to find one. It has been said that religion will call you to church to serve, but Jesus calls you to go into the world and serve. This was a truth I was learning about the hard way.

All in His Timing

> *Then the master said to the servant, "Go out to the roads and country lanes and compel them to come in, so that my house will be full."*
>
> —Luke 14:23

Because we were not able to find a church that we felt right about attending, we decided to embark on a journey and have our own services. We always invited a guest speaker/preacher to each meeting. When the weather was nice, we met outside underneath the trees. This went on for a couple of weeks until the family of one of the boys in the group started to attend. They were wealthy owners of a brick factory, and they had a large house, which they offered for us to use for our meetings. One of the speakers we invited frequently was scheduled to preach on a particular Sunday but had to cancel at the last minute, so we sang songs and had a testimony service, sharing what was on our hearts. It seemed like every Sunday at least one new parent started attending, and on that Sunday the father of two of the young ladies in the group, A Mr. Kurlow, visited. After the testimony service, he stood up and said, "Why don't we build our own church?" Everyone was confused about how we would do that; we had not been taking up much of a collection. We had approximately two hundred cruzeros (which equaled about two dollars), so how were we going to build a church? We had no money and no land.

It just so happened that we had been meeting near a piece of property that belonged to this very man. Mr. Kurlow explained, "I was going to sell this lot, but now I will give it to you to build a church." We were speechless! We could hardly believe what we had just heard! And, as if that blessing was not enough, the owner of the brick factory got on board and offered to give enough brick to build a building of a certain dimension—not large, but a nice size. Everyone was excited and praising God with hands uplifted, and first one and then another began to commit, saying, "I give *this*" or "I give *that.*" I was almost beside myself but managed to say, "Okay, now we need someone to build it for us." Hands began to go up: "I can come after work," "I am a carpenter," "I am a bricklayer," "I'm ___," or I'm ___". Everyone who had a skill (and some who did not) began to volunteer to come after work

Bill (top right) playing harmonica in a "worship band" formed by some of the young men in the fledgling church. They occasionally played on a local radio station, but Bill would put tape over the openings of the instrument so his mistakes could not be heard!

or on weekends or holidays, and we would build a church. What now? I did not know how to preach and did not know how to find someone who did. My speaking was geared toward the youth, not the church in general. So, we formed a board of directors.

News of our church spread rapidly, and only two months after being kicked out of our previous church, our congregation numbered approximately 150 to 200 souls. One man who had started to attend offered to render drawings of the building plan. He was a very smart man and had some skills in this area, although he was a dentist by profession. This was acceptable because we were not required to submit a lot of paperwork and obtain permits in Brazil, especially for building outside the city. After

Members of the new church gathered to see Bill and his family off to the United States.

approximately two months, we had built the walls and handmade benches, but the floor was dirt, and there was not yet a roof on the building. When my father heard what was happening, he started asking me each time I came back from a meeting, "What happened today?" I would say, "Well, *this* or *that* happened, and people donated, and we are going to start a church," I was surprised when he asked, "Has anyone donated the windows?" I told him they had not, so he said to put him down for donating the windows. Eventually, even my father started coming to the meetings!

While this was going on, I had been working on my papers to go to the United States. I had already been given a departure date of May 15, 1958, but I kept this a secret from everyone. I did not

Top: Bill visiting the church in Brazil almost 40 years after it was founded.
Bottom: (left and right) The church in Brazil as it was being built.

Mr. and Mrs. Kurlow, who donated land for the church to be built.

want anything to distract from the building of the church, and I wanted to be there to see it when it opened.

We had only one week until our scheduled opening, but the church still did not have a roof. On Friday night of the week that we were to open, we finally went to pick up the shingles, which were about four hours away by truck. We arrived too late; the warehouse had closed. We asked the locals where the boss of the suppliers lived. When we finally found him, he told us he did not have anyone working to help load the shingles. We talked him into opening the warehouse long enough for us to get them and load them ourselves. We returned to the church with the shingles around 2:00 p.m. on Saturday, and we started building the roof right away. It was finished by 1:00 a.m. on Sunday, the morning of our first service.

A lot of churches had been invited to the inauguration of our church, and the building, which measured only 100 feet × 50 feet, was filled to capacity! It was not until the Sunday following the inauguration that I told the church I would be departing for the United States in about two weeks or so. This news was heartbreaking: many were disappointed, and some even cried. My boss at the optical shop was not too happy about it either.

We had started trying to sell our house weeks before we were scheduled to leave because, at that time, it took cash to buy a house. No one went to the bank for a loan. We knew that very few people had enough cash to buy a house. We also knew if we waited until we had to leave it would push the value of the property down. It just so happened that a young couple who worked with my father was planning to marry, and they needed a home. They had the means to buy it for the asking price, and they did.

CHAPTER TEN

Coming to the USA

Your people will be my people, and your God my God.

—Ruth 1:16b

Enter Maria

On Saturday, May 15, 1958, approximately forty or fifty people came to the airport to see my family off. We finally made it to Kennedy Airport on Sunday evening, May 16th. As the plane circled low around the airport, I was amazed at all the lights on the roads, which were full of cars! I could not believe it . . . I had never seen that many lights or cars!

By the time we finally made it to church we were late, and the choir was singing. Of course, we were ushered down front. I was still looking for the nicest girls, naturally. When I saw Maria in the choir, I said to myself, "I think she is going to be the one." Fortunately for me, they did not require an audition to be in the choir, so I immediately joined! And when I finally got a job, I *made sure* it was at the same ring factory where Maria worked.

The church we attended was a little Ukrainian Assembly of God Church in Newark, New Jersey, and the people were very generous. They gave our family beds to sleep on and helped us to get settled into our new lives. We were there for a few weeks before my father decided to take us to visit my mother's uncle who lived in Herkimer, New York. My father's mindset was that he did not want to work in a factory, and that visit was all about buying a farm. Buying a farm was not going to be easy, because after selling our house and coming to the United States, we had only about one hundred US dollars. I had a total of five dollars in my pocket. Thankfully, my mother's uncle cosigned a note for us to buy a farm in a little town called New Port, just outside Utica, New York.

I was not happy with the situation at all. I still worked at the same factory as Maria, and I was trying to impress her so she would go out with me. She did not want to have much to do with me at first because it seemed like all I did was get into trouble. In addition to fixing and filing rings, one of my jobs was to change big canisters of oxygen that were used for soldering, sometimes changing them as often as two times a day. I would be summoned by a worker who needed a refill when he hit the empty container with something that made a loud clanking noise, and this would be my signal to pick it up and replace it with a full one.

On one occasion I retrieved a full tank from the warehouse but no matter how hard I tried; I could not get the cover off! I asked the guy next to me, "What do you use to open that?" I had never had problems getting the covers off the tanks before. He wanted to be a wise guy and said, "Oh, you use a hammer." Not knowing any better, I got a hammer from my desk and start to hammer it. Oh, boy! I was facing a big window of the office where the boss was sitting. Suddenly, I saw him jump from his chair, waving his hands and yelling, "Stop, stop!" I looked around to find everyone had left the building, fearing for their lives. I eventually figured it out and stopped banging, but the boss came in and yelled at me. Unfortunately (or fortunately, depending on how you look

Bill (3rd row, far right) and Maria (1st row, 2nd from right) in church choir shortly after migrating to the US

at it), I did not understand English very well at the time, and I had no clue what he was saying. Finally, I called a Puerto Rican man who worked there and asked him what was happening. He explained to me, "You cannot do that to the canister; it could cause an explosion, and people might get hurt or maybe even killed." I told my boss I did not know that would happen, and then I told him about the wise guy who had told me to use the hammer. He came and got the guy, took him to his office, kept him there, and "talked to him" for about a half-hour or so. That was just *one example* of the things that *did not* impress Maria.

Eventually, Maria started to accept me. However, when she found out I was going to move to a farm she said, "I *do not* want to go to a farm! I *do not* want to milk cows or anything else. I did that in Germany, and I *do not* want anything else to do with it!" I tried to convince her by telling her she would not have to, that she could stay in the house and cook, but she did not want any part of it. So, I made the four-hour drive to Newark in my old car every weekend to spend time with her. I finally convinced her I was the one, and we were engaged in September 1959. I continued to make trips to Newark to visit her whenever I could.

Spiritual Challenges Begin

> *The thief comes only to steal and kill and destroy; I have come that they may have life, and have it to the full.*
>
> —John 10:10

On Sunday, November 15, I was delivering milk to the milk house and crossed the same little bridge I had crossed many times. This time, however, the steering on the pickup truck failed, and I went over the bridge into the creek (which was a good 50 to 60 feet below). To make things worse, there was nothing under the water at the bottom of the creek but rocks. The truck landed upside down on the rocks, and the impact crushed the top of the cabin so that it was even with the seat! It just so happened that, as God would have it, the doors had flung open, and I had fallen partially out of the truck before it hit the water. I was temporarily stuck under the truck, but "Praise God!" I was able to pull free before the water covered the truck, so I was not drowned or crushed in the cabin. I suddenly realized I was standing in the middle of the creek all alone. I was trying to decide whether I was supposed to go to the farm (which was probably 10 to 15 minutes by foot) or go into town. I was finally able to climb out of the creek, and

I saw my neighbor coming down the road in his milk truck. He stopped and said, "What happened, what happened?" I told him I did not know what had happened, that I just went over the edge in the pickup truck. I had not noticed but my arm was bleeding badly. There was blood all over the truck, and there was a blood trail following me from the water to the bridge. He said, "Get into the truck; we have to take you to a doctor, *now!*"

There was only one real doctor in town—an old German doctor named Dr. Miller. We took off toward his house—only we really did not "take off" because my neighbor's truck could not "take off." The truck had eight cylinders and the trip was downhill but, unfortunately, only four of the cylinders were working. My neighbor finally put the truck in neutral, and it went faster down the hill than when it was in gear. When we finally made it to the doctor's house, his wife met us at the door and told us he was at the hospital. She insisted I come into the house so she could bandage my arm while she tried to get in touch with him. I was bleeding so badly that it did not take long for blood to soak through the bandage, but in the meantime, she had been able to get in touch with the doctor. He instructed me to get to the hospital immediately!

We looked around to see if there was anyone who could take me to the hospital, and there was no one. Most everyone was in church, and the church was outside town. We went out into the street, desperately trying to find someone passing by who could take me to the hospital. Finally, we spotted a state trooper who was headed in our direction, but we watched helplessly as he turned off the road one block before he reached us. One of the men standing in the street with us said he could run down the block and intercept him, which he did. The state trooper asked what had happened and then *he* tried to bandage my arm, but the blood continued to soak right through. He put his raincoat on me because the blood was dripping down my leg and sprinkling the seat. There was even blood on the window. I remember thinking that if I did not die from the truck accident, I probably would not survive the trip to the hospital. Anyway, unlike the truck, his patrol car was moving!

Dr. Miller was waiting for me at the hospital, and I was immediately put to sleep. I am not sure how long I was out of it, but when I woke up the doctor said, "Well, your arm is bad." Two younger doctors were suggesting amputation, but I told them, "No, give him a chance to try to fix it." Sure enough, the old German doctor agreed to perform surgery and after about a week, I was able to go home, along with my arm, which was in a sling. Praise God! My fingers may not have been working too well and I may not have been able to hold anything, but at least everything was in its place . . . the bottom of my arm was still connected to the top of my arm.

Spiritual Challenges Continue

> *The Lord will keep you from all harm—he will watch over your life; the Lord will watch over your coming and going both now and forevermore.*
>
> —Ps. 121:7–8

It was early in December and Maria was anxious to see me after the accident, so she came with friends from Newark to visit for a few days. She was not happy when the time came for her to go home, but she was able to visit the doctor before she left. He told her not to worry and assured her that everything would be okay. Maria's sister, Christa, called me a week or so after they left to tell me that Maria, herself, was not doing well. She had been to a doctor and was diagnosed with a virus. The doctor told them it was nothing too serious and not to worry. They had planned to come to the farm on Christmas Eve, but she had continued to get worse. I managed to get a ride and went to visit her in New Jersey, instead. She was too sick and lethargic to even look at the presents I had brought for her. She was very lethargic and just lying there with a high fever. We called the doctor and he instructed us to take her to the hospital immediately. After several tests, they determined her appendix had burst—a condition that most people did not survive at that time. I stayed for as long as I could, but after a couple of days, I had to go back to the farm. It was so hard to leave her at the hospital, but I had no choice. Once I was back at the farm, her sister called me and said the doctor wanted to do surgery in a week to ten days.

It just so happened that, as God would have it, the doctor had gone to New York for a convention where he met another German doctor, and they had discussed Maria's case. He admitted to his colleague that he was not sure if he was doing the right thing, but that he had scheduled the surgery for when he returned. The doctor from Germany said, "No way, not yet! Use antibiotics to try to get all the infection into one spot, and then do the surgery. It may take a week or two but don't do the surgery until the infection is under control because it could be fatal." When her doctor returned, he required Maria to sign papers stating that waiting was not what he had recommended, but that she wanted to be treated the way the other doctor had suggested. Sure enough, after about a week or so, she was released from the hospital after being treated only with antibiotics.

Wedded Bliss

> *There is a time for everything, and a season for every activity under the heavens.*
>
> —Eccles. 3:1

Before my accident and Maria's unexpected illness, we had scheduled a wedding day for mid-February 1960, and many things had already been done to prepare for the wedding. Maria's sisters had worked so hard! The invitations had already been sent with the place and time for the reception, and all the deposits had been paid, but Maria did not want to get married in her condition. She knew she would be having surgery soon, and she wanted to cancel the wedding, but her doctor encouraged her to go ahead with it and assured her that everything was going to be okay. So, we were married on February 13, 1960, as planned. The wedding went well, and we went to the farm afterward, but neither of us felt very well. We were in touch with the doctor in Newark and he informed us that he had scheduled Maria's surgery for March. Sure enough, she went through the surgery fine, and the doctor told her, "Only with the help of God could everything go so well." We returned to the farm, and she was still weak but continued to get better.

I tried to help my father with the farm, but I could not do much with one arm. I still had no strength in my hand and could not even hold a pencil in my fingers. I said to my father, "Look, neither of us can do much for you at the farm, and you need help." I suggested to him that my brother-in-law (who had married my sister a year or so earlier) come help him, and Maria and I would go back to Newark. My father was not too happy about it, but he needed help and he eventually agreed.

CHAPTER ELEVEN

Life Lived in Between

The Lord is good to those whose hope is in him, to the one who seeks him.

—Lam. 3:25

The Right Connections

We moved into my mother-in-law's house, and Maria continued to improve. Fortunately, it was not long before she was able to find a job sitting behind a desk. It just so happened that her new job was inspecting hinges for eyeglasses in an eyeglass factory! I am so blessed when I think how God always sees down the road—past anything I could ever imagine. Only *He* could foresee the role that skill would play in our ministry years later.

Slowly, my arm started to improve, so I began looking for work but jobs were hard to come by. One day Maria came to me and said, "You know what my boss asked me today?" He had asked her what I did for a living, and she had told him I was an optician by trade, and that I was currently searching for work. She went on to ask if he would be willing to interview me for a possible job opening, and he agreed. The interview went well. He asked me several questions and then he placed ten to twelve hinges on the desk in front of me and said, "What is wrong with those hinges?" I could see immediately what was wrong; the machine was set to the wrong cut for the barrels and thickness. He must have decided that I was capable enough because, after the interview, he asked if I would be interested in working for him as a foreman on the night shift. The factory ran 24 hours a day, and the night foreman was scheduled to retire in about three months. It just so happened that they had not yet found the right person to replace him. Maria's boss said he felt sure I would be able to do the job after a little training, and I accepted the position.

In the beginning, I trained during the day and worked the same hours as Maria, but after a couple of weeks, I began training on the night shift with the night foreman. We fell into a schedule where Maria would work the day shift, come home, give me the car, and then I would go back to work the night shift at the same place. This became difficult for a couple of reasons. First, we only saw each other when we were trading out the car and on the weekends. Second, I got no sleep. Maria's mother's house was located about a half-block away from the school, and our bedroom was at the front of the house facing the street. As soon as I lay down and barely fell asleep, the kids would walk by on their way to school, yelling and making a lot of noise. After it finally got quiet again, I would have a hard time getting back to sleep, and sometimes I never could!

This went on for maybe a month before I came home one day and said, "I just can't take it anymore." Instead of trying to go to sleep, I got out the telephone book (what we used to find phone numbers and addresses before we had smartphones) and I found three listings under *"optical."* I decided to visit each address. The shop at the first address had been closed, and the building was scheduled to be demolished. The second address was a wholesale optical business that was owned by three brothers. They said that they were looking for an optician to fit eyeglasses, and I spent three or four hours talking with them before they finally hired me. The brothers treated me very well, and life was quiet for a time until we were surprised and blessed with our first child, Rick. Our new working arrangements made taking care of a baby a little bit different and a lot challenging, but life went on and was good.

Preparation for a Calling

We visited different churches, and many people from different congregations began to prophesy over us that we would eventually end up doing mission work. We had our second child, Cindy, and people we did not even know continued to tell us that we would go into ministry on the mission field. Each time this happened, I looked at the children and thought to myself, *"People, are you sure you know what you're saying?"* How could I do mission work with the children as small as they were? Besides, I had never gone to Bible school. My understanding of what was required to go into mission work consisted of going to Bible school for a couple of years, learning another language, and then being sent to another country to preach wherever they put you. Time passed, and our third child, Sharon, was born.

The company I worked for had allowed me to open a small optical shop in the front of my house while I continued to work for them. We became active in ministry to missionaries and when missionaries visited the church, we always volunteered to open our home to them. The pastor would send them to our house to stay for a night, two nights, or sometimes even a week. It was also always my pleasure to help them with eyeglasses whenever I could. Meanwhile, Maria and I continued to have similar encounters with *different* people in *different* places—all prophesying that we would go into ministry.

A Faithful Example

> *I will instruct you and teach you in the way you should go; I will counsel you with my loving eye on you.*
>
> —Ps. 32:8

One day, a missionary who was doing missions—mostly in Ukraine and parts of Russia—visited our church and stayed with us for about a week. His mission was to smuggle Bibles, which he did by putting a few Bibles in the bottom of his suitcase and covering them with clothes. He had already been stopped several times, and what few Bibles he had were immediately confiscated even though he had claimed that they were for his own use. The time came for him to prepare for his next trip to Ukraine, and he placed twenty-four Bibles in the bottom of his suitcase. He covered them with papers and then covered the papers with clothes. Before he left, he noticed some of the sunglasses in my shop and said, "Oh, these are so nice. May I try some?" Since he admired them so much, I offered for him to take some for himself. This made him so happy! He explained that sometimes he would lose his sunglasses, and sometimes he gave them to ministers who were already serving there. I encouraged him to take some with him, and he happily agreed to take about five or six pairs.

The missionary left for Ukraine and when his plane landed, he was taken immediately to the checkpoint. Security there was unpredictable but for some reason, it was especially strict on that day. Sometimes, they simply asked if you are carrying this thing or that thing; sometimes they forced you to take everything out of your suitcase. This was one of those "*take everything out of your suitcase*" days. The missionary thought his goose was cooked because he knew if they found as many Bibles as he was carrying this time, he would surely be thrown into jail!

When his turn came to go through security, the inspector (who was wearing sunglasses) asked him what was in his suitcase, and the missionary told him it was his clothes. The inspector noticed the sunglasses the missionary was wearing and said, "Those are nice sunglasses you have. Can you see well with them?" The missionary said, "Yes, I can see very well with them. Would you like to try them?" The inspector put on the glasses and said, "These are *very* nice!" The missionary quickly saw an opportunity and said, "Well, I have extra glasses, so you can have these if you'd like." Sure enough, he was so pleased with the glasses that he told the missionary to put his clothes back in the suitcase and just go ahead and pass through. The missionary knew that God's hand was on that encounter because he knew if he had taken everything out of the suitcase, the Bibles would surely have been found, and that would be especially sad in this case. You see, the reason *these* Bibles were so valuable is they were to be given to a pastor who had an old Bible that he was trying to share with other pastors. He had been doing this by copying one page at a time by hand and then passing that page along to the next pastor so that God's Word could be shared.

Family Obligations

> *Start children off on the way they should go, and even when they are old they will not turn from it.*
>
> —Prov. 22:6

We began to attend a Ukrainian Assembly of God church regularly, but there were many Brazilians and Argentinians who attended and translation was difficult. When we asked the kids what they learned in Sunday school, they could not tell us because they did not understand the language, and it was confusing for them. Rick started having difficulties once school started as well. It was a *bad school* in a *bad area* with lots of *bad kids*. He often came home crying because they had taken his lunch and so on. There were no doors on the restrooms at school, so he would come running home and go straight to the bathroom because he had not gone all day. We went to the school and complained, but we were told there was nothing that could be done because the school was integrated. We began thinking about moving to a better area but in the meantime, we changed to an American church for the sake of the kids. We liked the church, and we became good friends with a particular couple who had a little girl about Ricky's age. However, the church was the only thing that was keeping us there, so soon we decided it was time to move on.

I had enjoyed living on the farm in upstate New York, and I especially liked Albany. I told my boss things were not working out for us, and we planned to move back. I assured him that I loved my job and the decision had nothing to do with it; the problem was everything else. It just was not a good place to raise the kids. I reserved a U-Haul for a Saturday morning and we were going to move, but on the Friday before we planned to leave, two of the bosses called me into the office and asked me why I was going—why this, why that, and were we sure we wanted to move? I told them I was going to pick up the truck on my way home, and we planned to leave for Albany the next morning. One of the bosses said, "How about if we give you another $50 per week?" Wow, that hit me hard because at that time (1964) $50 per week was good money! I said, "Let me take a few minutes to think about it." He told me to go into his office and think about it and to call my wife to discuss it. I called Maria and she said, "What are we going to do? Everything is packed to go!" We were living in a six-family home that we owned together with my father, and I had already rented my part out. I continued to struggle because it was good money, but I told Maria I thought we should still go. She said, "I don't know . . ."

We were both on the verge of crying, and not only about the money. We would be leaving her mother and my parents, and we would be moving to an area almost four hours away from anyone we knew. Eventually, the bosses came into the room and I told them I would stay. I called Maria again and said, "Maria, we are staying." This made her happy, but she said, "Now what are we going to do? Where are we going to stay?" We had already rented out our apartment. Eventually, everything worked out.

We stayed and continued to attend the American church, but the area did not get any better. I talked to a friend who worked at a machine shop making cams, which was something not many people had the skills to do. He had been offered a job at a location in South Jersey—almost in Philadelphia. He said, "I'm going on Sunday to meet the boss. Would you like to come with me?" I had visited there once before and all I could remember about the area was chicken houses and a *bad* odor, but I agreed to go with him to a town called Medford. It turned out that Medford was a nice area, so I changed my mind about the chicken houses. I decided to look for a job there. I spent a couple of weekends putting in applications for jobs in the area, but nothing ever came up. The time came for my friend to talk to his boss and tell him for sure whether he was going to take the job or not. He decided to take the job and move because it was a good offer in a good area. He said to me, "I'll move now, and later you can move." I told him this was the last weekend I was going to look for a job there before giving up. I looked but I found nothing.

When I returned home, I checked my phone messages and there was one from a Mr. Becker, saying, "You applied for a job, and I am interested in talking to you." Since my previous employer was named "Baker," I was very confused. Becker, Baker . . . it was all the same to me! I called the number he had left on the answering machine, and I asked where he was from. He said, "I am from Willingboro," which is close to Medford. Sure enough, God had worked it out and answered our prayers yet again. Two days later, I was hired by Mr. Becker to work in the optical department at McGuire Air Force Base. Praise God! He protects us when we do not even realize it. How many times has He proven that His plan is perfect and all He asks of us is to have faith? We loaded everything up again and moved. The kids were happy there, and it was almost like life was starting anew for us. Except . . . everywhere we went, new people prophesied over us that our ministry would be to serve in missions.

I was happy at my job at McGuire AFB for about a year and a half, and then things changed. My boss lost the contract with the military, and the shop had to move off the base. A couple of months before that time, I had asked him if I could open an optical shop in my house. I had all the equipment, but it was quite far away from the shop and that meant I would have to work in the evenings when I got home. He said, "As long as it doesn't interfere with this job, that's fine." So I opened my little place at home and got a little bit of business here and there. A couple of weeks after the office at the base closed, my boss offered me a job in the shop at the main office. I started working there but soon discovered he did not need another person; the place was not that busy. I had heard that Sears Optical was looking for part-time opticians, so I talked to my boss and he said if I wanted to, I should go check it out. I was hired part-time at Sears Optical, working two evenings a week. I was working for my boss a little bit, and I was working for Sears Optical a little bit, and I was doing okay.

One Sunday, we were visiting the next town, which was called Medford Lakes. It was a small but nice community, and it had many beautiful lakes. A little store on the main street was for rent, so I checked into it and found the lease was very affordable. I thought maybe I could move the shop from my house and open it there, and that is what I did. In the beginning, I was only there a couple of evenings a week and then at Sears a couple of evenings a week. Before long, God blessed me greatly, and my shop grew so fast that I had to quit Sears and work full time at my shop. A good friend who dispensed hearing aids started working part-time for me, and we expanded to include a Miracle Ear franchise. Soon there was enough business for him to work full time. We ended up staying there for more than eight years, beginning in 1973, and God blessed that business greatly.

CHAPTER TWELVE

Thirst for Missions

Wait on the Lord: be of good courage, and he shall strengthen thine heart: wait, I say, wait on the Lord.

—Ps. 27:14 (KJV)

Maria Makes Connections

We began traveling to Teen Challenge in Pennsylvania to provide eyeglasses for needy children. Sometimes, I was able to go into homes to minister, and God helped us greatly to do this. I became more involved at the church we attended. It seemed like every time there was a need, we were ready and able to help. The pastor suggested that I get a pastor's license, which I did, and then I was able to help even more. When we were at home, we always invited people over for dinner after church so that Maria could minister to them with her *great* gift of cooking. God blessed us with our next child, Mark. Despite all this, somehow our hearts were still in missions.

In the meanwhile, an organization based out of Florida, which is called "The Book of Life," came to our church and made a presentation. They were trying to organize a group of people to go to Ukraine and Russia to give out little New Testament Bibles in the schools in their native language. I was a little interested in going, but I backed out because I was so busy with so many things. It just so happened that they changed their mission from Ukraine to Belarus, the part of Poland where I was born. That got my attention and I could not turn it down, so we decided to go.

The trip was uneventful and once we arrived, we were organized into four groups of five people each. We went into the schools where the kids were assembled, shared the gospel with them, and gave them booklets. We invited them to come to an evening service, which had been arranged to take place in a big theater with a large seating capacity. When I gave the booklets to the kids, I noticed some of them kept bringing the booklets closer in, further out, closer in, and then further out again. After a while, I noticed almost *all* the kids were doing the same thing. I asked them why they were doing this, and their answer was simply, "We can't see it." They also complained of some throat problems. You see, the name of the town we were visiting was Molodechno, and during the explosion at Chernobyl several years earlier, the radiation fallout and smoke had passed directly over the town. The hospital there was still full of children who had been affected by it. Even at the hospital, the children were constantly saying, "I can't see . . . I can't see." We returned home determined to go back and provide eyeglasses, but it seemed like everything we tried did not work out. Then I started having dreams at night . . . almost like visions. I heard the voices of the children saying, "I can't see . . . I can't see!"

Maria had gone to a prayer meeting one night after we returned from Belarus. I had stayed home because mostly ladies attended, and sometimes they prayed for hours! It was not unusual for Maria to get home after 11:00 p.m. That night I waited up for her, and eventually fell asleep after she got home, and I began to dream again. The voices and the faces of the children were more real than ever, but this time I heard a voice like I had never heard before. It was not human, and there is no way to explain it, but it asked me twice, "What are you going to do about it?" Then it stopped. I woke up to Maria asking me what was wrong because I had been so restless that I was hitting and kicking and striking out for no apparent reason. I had never told her about my dreams, so I tried to explain them and how real they had been on that night. Then I told her about the voice asking me what I was going to do about it. She looked at me and said, "Well, what *are* you going to do about it?" I said, "I don't know; I don't know." Over a month passed, and I did not have the dream or hear the voice again.

One day I was watching television when the *700 Club* program came on. Their mission department (Operation Blessing) was advertising to build a flying hospital, and they were looking for volunteers, so I wrote down the telephone number. A couple of months passed, and I lost the number and forgot all about it.

Coming Full Circle

> *Faithful is he that calleth you, who also will do it*
>
> —1 Thess. 5:24 (KJV)

The day came when we were notified that the pastor of the Ukrainian church that sponsored us had passed away. We attended the funeral where we met a good friend of the pastor, a missionary. After World War II when the Americans had taken over Germany, this pastor had visited camps to minister to the refugees and helped build churches. It just so happened that he knew Maria from Germany! He was seated next to me and said,

"How are things going for you here?" Of course, I responded, "Oh, everything is fine." After a few minutes of silence, he looked at me and I said, "No, it's not fine." The noise in the room was so loud that we could hardly hear each other so he suggested we go into the sanctuary to talk. Once we were in the sanctuary, I told him about my dreams. He looked at me and said, "You know God is calling you." I said, "Well, I know God is calling me, but what should I do? I try, and all the doors slam in my face!" Then he asked me if I had heard about The Flying Hospital and Operation Blessing on the 700 Club. I said, "Yeah, I saw on TV where they were going to build an airplane. I even took the number down and then lost it, so I never followed up on it." He simply told me, "God has His timing for everything. We can go downstairs and fellowship now." So, he got up and turned to me and said, "They will call you." Then he walked away to join the others and left me sitting there. I felt even worse than before because I thought I was going to find some answers, but instead, I felt I had just been pushed away. I finally got up and joined the others and when Maria saw me, she asked what had happened. I told her about the conversation and that I still did not have any answers.

Sure enough, about a week after the funeral I received a letter from Operation Blessing. The letter started with an introduction: "I'm Paul Williams, and I'm in charge of The Flying Hospital. Brother ______ talked to you and explained to me that you are interested in doing short-term missions. I understand that you are an optician, and that is exactly what we need. I would like to discuss this further with you if you are interested." Right away, I contacted him and said, "Yes, yes! Where is your place?" He explained that their headquarters was in Virginia Beach. I had never been there, but I had seen the *700 Club* program once or twice. I got the address and phone number and asked when

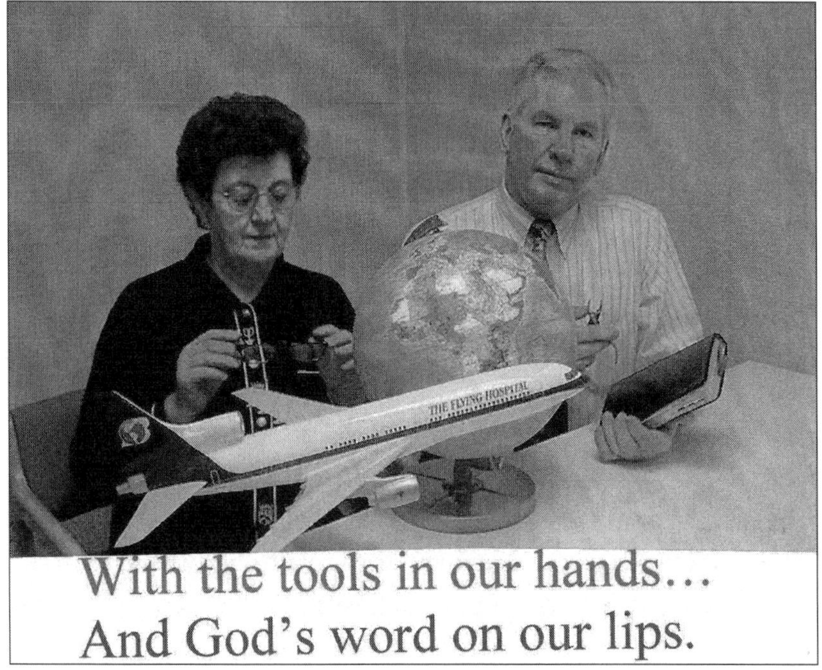

THE FLYING HOSPITAL
With the tools in our hands…
And God's word on our lips.

Found in a scrapbook, Maria (left) and Bill (right) pictured with a model of CBN Ministry's Flying Hospital.

would be a good time for me to come see him. The letter had come on a Monday, and he said, "How about Wednesday?" I said, "Great! I'll be there." Wednesday came and I closed my shop and made my way to the *700 Club* headquarters to meet him. He first gave me a tour of the facility and then he explained to me the need for an optician to make and supply eyeglasses. He asked, "What can you do?" I said, "I can take an entire lab and make eyeglasses on the premises." He said, "Could you really?!" I was curious about the size of the plane, so he explained that it would be at the New Jersey airport in two weeks so I could see it for myself. He pulled two tickets from a drawer and said, "Here are tickets to attend the inaugural dinner and visit the airplane."

I was so anxious to see the airplane that two weeks felt like two months. When the day finally came, I was not disappointed because it was a thing of beauty! It was an L-1011 wide-bodied jet that had been converted into a hospital. It was designed to carry missionaries and medical staff all over the world, along with complete exam rooms, equipment, and operating rooms. To say that Maria and I were excited to take our first trip on the Flying Hospital would be an understatement.

It was 1996 when we took our first trip on the Flying Hospital to Ukraine. I was amazed at how God blessed that ministry. We were just as excited each time another trip was scheduled, and we could not wait to go! Unfortunately, this meant every time I went on a trip, I had to close my business and put a sign on the door stating I had gone on a humanitarian medical trip. I was either supplying frames or asking for donations from the manufacturers I normally did business with, and thankfully, they were giving me just enough for each trip.

Confirmation

> *Now to him who is able to do immeasurably more than all we ask or imagine, according to his power that is at work within us, to him be glory in the church and in Christ Jesus throughout all generations, for ever and ever! Amen.*
>
> —Eph. 3:20–21

After some time had passed, I was contacted by a man from the Lions Club in a nearby town. He said he had heard about our missions, and he wanted to know if we could come there to do a presentation of what it was all about. I told him I would be glad to do it, and we set a date. When the day finally came, I set up my display in the room where we were meeting. I showed them what we did, what we needed, and what all was involved in making it happen. They were impressed with the setup. After the meeting we had dinner, and two men joined us at our table. One of them asked if I needed frames for my missions. It just so happened that he "might" have someone who could help with that. He asked for my telephone number, and he told me that someone would be in touch.

I was working in the shop a couple of days later when I received a telephone call. The man on the other end of the line introduced himself and told me which company and warehouse he was from, confirming he was the person the gentleman at the Lions Club dinner had mentioned. He proceeded to tell me that he had approximately 35,000 frames that he would like to donate. I could not believe it! I asked, "How many . . . 3,500?" to which he replied, "No, no; I said 35,000." I almost fell from the chair I was sitting in. The frames were in Camden, New Jersey, which was only a twenty-minute drive from my home. He told me I was welcome to come to see them any time, so I asked him if I could come in the next day or two. He gave me the full address and told me he would see me the next day.

When I arrived at the warehouse, he took me behind one of the big doors, and I saw fourteen pallets of boxes—all wrapped in plastic. He cut one of the boxes and opened it up. I was surprised to see that the glasses were all brand new, still in their plastic envelopes. I asked if they were all like the one that he showed me, and he said, "No, there are also some plastic frames." I told him, "I will take them!!" Then he said, "Well, there is one little problem."

I *knew* it had to be too good to be true. The man continued, "I have another large shipment coming in on Friday, and I will need this space. If you do not take them by that time, they will all go into the dumpster." It was Wednesday. I said, "No, no, no . . . don't do that! Give me until tomorrow." He said that would be fine, but he wanted them gone by Friday. For the entire trip home, I wondered what I was going to do. Where would I get a truck? If I could get a truck and actually go get the frames, where was I going to put them? My house did not even have a garage! I was so distracted by my thoughts that I passed the exit to my house.

> *We ought therefore to show hospitality to such people so that we may work together for the truth.*
>
> —3 John 1:8

Finally, the thought occurred to me that I should call Operation Blessing, which I did. My good friend and the director of the program, Ron Oates, greeted me and asked how I had been doing. I said to him, "Fine, but I have a little bit of a problem. I have received a donation of 35,000 frames, and I have no place to put them." I was surprised when he said, "No problem! We can even send a truck from Virginia Beach to pick them up if we need to." I told him I would appreciate anything he could do to help because I had no way to get them and nowhere to put them, but I knew if we did not do something with them soon, those shiny new frames were going to end up in the garbage! He told me to give him a few minutes, and he would call me back, which he did. "Bill, it just so happens that we have a truck in Philadelphia right now, picking up some food donations. I will give your telephone number to the driver, and he can call you to give him directions to the warehouse. He will let you know what time he can be there."

Ron told me to stand by the telephone and wait for the driver's call. It was only ten to fifteen minutes before the call came. I was happy to hear the voice of my friend, Israel, on the other end of the line. Israel and I knew each other well because we had worked together packing boxes for previous mission trips. When I told him the address he said, "Oh, I know the area well. Tell him I'll be there in about an hour." I told him I would meet him there. I called my contact at the warehouse and asked him if we could pick up the frames in about an hour. He said that would be great! I told him a truck was headed his way from Operation Blessing and that I was also going to try to be there around the same time. I jumped into my car and drove to the warehouse as fast as I could, and I arrived just in time to see the truck backing up to the doors! Israel loaded the truck and took off with the frames, but I stayed behind to thank the man for the donation and his kindness. As soon as I pulled out of the parking lot, tears built up in my eyes—so much that I could hardly see to drive. I understood a little bit more about how great God is. I understood that when He calls you, he will provide everything you need to be obedient to the call.

God blessed us mightily as we were able to travel on many, many mission trips after that. I continued to receive calls from the warehouse, asking me to come pick up more. Each time, they donated around 10,000 to 15,000 eyeglasses! Thank God for everything!

CHAPTER THIRTEEN

Joy in Serving

Serve the Lord with gladness: come before his presence with singing.

—Ps. 100:2 (KJV)

It's About Time!

A great day came in September 1996 when it was time for our first trip to Kiev, Ukraine. It was an exciting day when we left, but even more exciting once we arrived! We were on a mission to an area where we would be able to use a language we knew. We would be able to communicate with the people to better help fit them with glasses and more importantly, to better pray for their needs. We were amazed to witness many miracles and see how God answered prayers on that trip.

The next mission was to Almaty, Kazakhstan, and it was interesting too. I will never forget a father and mother who brought their eight-year-old son to the second floor of the clinic where we were working. They told us he was having difficulty at school and that he could not see far off. After he was examined and received glasses, I pointed to the vision chart on the wall and asked him to read it. Instead of looking at the chart, he directed his eyes to the window and would not look away. While I waited for a reaction from him, his father asked him, "What's the matter, can't you see?" Suddenly, he became excited and exclaimed, "I see leaves in the trees! I see! I see leaves in the trees!" Then he read the whole chart.

On the last day of the mission, a large dinner was prepared for everyone. During the dinner, all the missionaries gave reports about what they had done and had seen and the miracles they had witnessed. The evening was concluded by singing worship songs. During the singing, an elderly man who had been working in the optical department with me jumped from his seat and started to sing and dance. He was jumping and dancing like a 20-year-old man! He finally stopped to say, "Praise God! Praise God! When I decided to come on this mission, I asked God to help me see at least 40 to 50 souls come to faith in God. Guess what? God helped me to bring 110 souls to Christ!" Before it was over, we were all jumping and dancing and singing and praising God for this mission.

> *The Lord hath done great things for us; whereof we are glad.*
>
> —Ps. 126:3 (KJV)

Our next mission was to Bolivia. There, a baby girl who was maybe one to two years old was brought to us; she was almost completely blind. Her mother had somehow managed to obtain a prescription for her glasses but could not afford to buy them. The prescription called for such high refractive power that I did not think we had anything even near to it. We tried a few of the glasses we had on hand, but nothing seemed to work for her. No matter what we tried, she did not appear to see anything at all. As we tried first one pair and then another, she became impatient and started to resist our experiments. Finally, Maria said,

"Wait a minute! Do you remember the pair of glasses that a lady brought to us as a donation from her daughter?" I told her that I did remember them, that they were very small glasses, with very strong power. I had put them in the box to take with us, but then I had taken them out because I did not think I would ever be able to use them. Maria—as only Maria can—said, "Well, I felt like I needed to put them back in the box, so I did." I was doubtful so I told her if she put them in the box then she should find them and bring them to me.

Sure enough, she found them. They measured a high power, approximately 12 to 13 diopters. I told the child's mother to hold her and I would try to put the glasses on her. The mother, at this point, was giving up because the little girl had pulled off everything we had tried. I told her I thought her baby just might keep these on (I said this in faith, knowing that children tend to pull them off most of the time). Despite her doubt, the mother decided to cooperate and continued to hold the child in her lap. As I put the glasses on the child's face, I was not even sure if she could see light. After several tries, we eventually got the glasses on her face correctly, and I held her hands to keep her from swatting them off.

Suddenly, I felt her relax her little hands as she started to move her head, looking all around the room. The more she began to see, the calmer she became. She had been facing away from her mother, who was crying softly because she was beginning to realize her baby could see. Slowly, the child turned around until she was facing her mother. The little girl looked at her mother for what seemed like a full minute before she started to smile. Then she reached out her hands and began to caress her mother's face. There were about fifteen people in the room—roughly 30

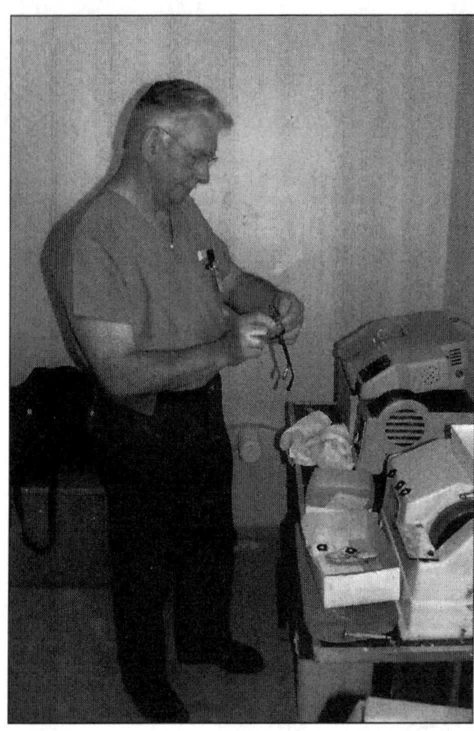

Bill making glasses on the flying hospital.

eyes—and not one of them was dry. Not ours, not the translators, and not even the other patients who were waiting to be fitted for glasses. Crying and praising God could be heard throughout the room because, for the first time in her life, this baby girl could see her mother's face.

Friendships and Opportunities

> *I always thank my God for you because of his grace given you in Christ Jesus.*
>
> —1 Cor. 1:4

The trip to Nairobi, Kenya, was an interesting one because this is where we first met Dr. Lance Haluka, optometrist and our dear friend. He was a lot of fun, and he was great with the children. Wherever you saw a group of kids having fun, you could count on Lance to be at the center of it. He could encourage anyone around him with his sense of humor and his servant's heart, which was obvious to anyone who worked with him. That was the first of many trips we would enjoy serving and fellowshipping together with him and his wife, Debbie.

Once we left Nairobi, we traveled for about two hours until we reached a village in the middle of nowhere. There were about 200 mud huts, a good-sized church, and a couple of unfinished Bible school buildings off to the side—one of which was assigned to us as living quarters. Early in the morning of the first day, we woke to find thousands of people waiting! Where did they all come from?!

Unfortunately, there had been an extremely dry season a year or two before, and everything around us was dry. We did not even have water to take a shower. On one of the hottest days, we were sweating and not smelling so good, and we *really* needed a shower by the end of the day. There *was* a shower but it was doing no one any good because no water had been in it for quite some time. I decided to go check it out anyway, and I was so happy to see water trickling out of the faucet! I quickly got under it long enough to get wet, turn it off, and then thoroughly soap myself. I turned the faucet back on expecting to rinse off when—you guessed it—the trickle had stopped. I had to use my bottle of drinking water to finish rinsing.

The mosquitoes were unbelievable there! The menu was a choice of stew or stew. We ate unrefrigerated stew every day for a week. We joked about it every evening, wondering what was new or different from the stew we had the day before. Dr. Haluka would joke and say something like, "There are a couple more flies in it tonight than there was last night" (or maybe mosquitoes). We had to have strong stomachs to eat that stew! The accommodations may not have been great, but we had a great time!

Monkeys and Cocktails

> *Thou shalt not bear false witness against thy neighbour.*
>
> —Exod. 20:16 (KJV)

We were in Kenya for two weeks, and on the first weekend, we were treated to a safari. When we reached our lunch destination, we found they had prepared a nice buffet with all kinds of food, including salad and vegetables, and raw fruits, which were not available at the camp. We had been told to be careful about eating raw foods because we could get sick from the water the locals used to wash them. Some of us chose not to eat the food, but others took the chance and, unfortunately, regretted it. Everyone who ate the uncooked food became sick.

We separated into different groups to see the animals after lunch. I went outside the building and found a patio with tables and chairs, which seemed like a peaceful area to rest and take in the sights. It was not too long before two fancy ladies came along, well-dressed and delicately carrying their mixed drinks in their hands. They chose a table and carefully placed their drinks down

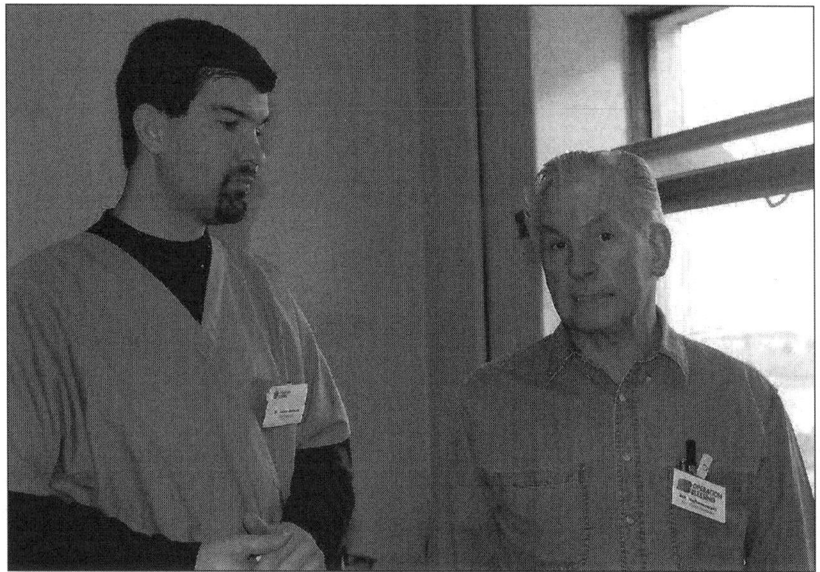

Lance Haluka, optometrist (left) and Bill Wojtaskzewski, optician (right).

before walking to look over the wall at the animals. I was sitting there, just minding my own business, when a monkey appeared out of nowhere! He ran to their table and I could not believe my eyes as he took one of the drinks, gulped it down, and then put the glass back on the table. Then, I watched in amazement as he took the second drink, gulped *that one* down, and then put the glass back on the table—just like the first one. Before I knew what had happened, the monkey took off and disappeared into the trees!

Suddenly it dawned on me what the fancy ladies might think about what had happened to their drinks. Sure enough, when they returned to their table and saw the empty glasses, they stared directly at me! I told them, "It was the monkey . . . the monkey did it!" They kept looking at me with sarcastic expressions, as if to say, *"Sure, sure . . . the monkey did it!"* Oh well. That was not the first time or the last time I would be blamed for something I did not do.

Enemies and Opportunities

> *"You have heard that it was said, 'Love your neighbor and hate your enemy.' But I tell you, love your enemies and pray for those who persecute you."*
>
> —Matt. 5:43–44

A trip was scheduled to go to Siberia at the end of September 1999. Two days before we were to leave, Maria waited on a gentleman in the shop who could not hear very well. She took his history to find out why his hearing was impaired, and this was his story: He had been in Pinsk (my hometown) during the war, and he had been a member of the Partisan party. He told Maria exactly where and when he had been there, but he had no idea it was at the exact same time and the exact same place my parents had been held prisoner—where my parents were supposed to have been executed. Right away Maria said, "Wait a minute. Come with me because someone would like to meet you."

I was taking care of other customers at a table in another corner of the shop. I had more than a dozen hearing aids in stock at the time and I thought I could help the man, so I said, "Okay, tell me what happened." He told me he lost his hearing because he had been beaten many times while in prison. I asked him why he was in prison, and he told me his story. He explained that after the war when Russia took power, the Partisans were sent to prison in different parts of Siberia because they were not trusted "for some reason." After fitting him with a hearing aid, I could better communicate with him, and we continued our conversation. I asked him where exactly he had been in Pinsk and, sure enough, he told me he had been in a town called Mohro. Immediately, my blood pressure shot straight up, and I felt my face flush. I knew that was where my parents had been kept prisoner while waiting to be executed. At first, I felt like putting my hands around his neck, but then the Holy Spirit reminded me of the commandment of Jesus to "love your enemies."

After I calmed down a little bit, I explained to him that my parents had been held prisoner there. He responded, "Oh, I probably wasn't there at the same time." It was obvious that he had become extremely uncomfortable, and he decided to leave right away. Maria confessed that she was not surprised when I told her what had happened. It is almost as if she knew it was God's timing for me to face my emotions and to make peace with what had happened.

The next day I was surprised to see the same man return to the clinic, and he came straight to the table where I was working! I thought maybe the hearing aid was not working well for him because sometimes it takes a while to learn how to use them properly. He told me that everything was working fine, that he had come to see me. Then he reached into his pocket and took out a medal. He handed me the medal and I asked him, "What is this?" He told me it was a medal he had been awarded for his service during the war. "I would like you to have this so that you don't forget me," he said. I told him not to worry, that I would *never* forget him. So here we were, many years later, thousands of miles away, and I met one of the men who had been in the same place where my parents were held as prisoners to be executed.

More Friendships and Opportunities

> *Who is our brother and co-worker in God's service in spreading the gospel of Christ, to strengthen and encourage you in your faith.*
>
> —1 Thess. 3:2b

The week before we left for Krasnoyarsk and Bratsk, we went to the Operation Blessing warehouse in Virginia Beach to pack all the supplies we thought we would need for the missions at both locations. We arrived in Krasnoyarsk and set up the clinic. Everything was going smoothly except for the extreme cold, snow, and ice. After a couple of days, we realized we were in short supply of glasses in two specific strengths (prescriptions) that we could not find, no matter how hard we looked. The pharmacist, John Lynd, had been given the task of ordering glasses, medicine, and other supplies. He helped us look for the boxes that held the specific glasses, but by the end of the day, he had been unable to find them either.

We were surprised the next morning when a box that had only a couple of pairs left the night before was completely *full* of glasses in the specific strengths that were missing. We called John again and said, "John, are you playing games with us?" He said, "I don't know what you are talking about." We used the new glasses, and by the end of the day, the box was empty again. The next morning when we returned to the clinic, we found the box was full again. We asked John if he was responsible, again. He assured us he just *could not* understand it! He called the warehouse in Virginia Beach to ask if they saw any boxes that were supposed to come with us to Russia, thinking some may have been left behind. Sure enough, a few boxes of glasses in this strength had been pushed to the side and were never loaded on the airplane; they were still in Virginia Beach. For the remainder of the trip, each day we came to the clinic we found a box full of glasses in the strengths we needed.

Once again, we realized how great our God is! He never lets us down. Sometimes, He uses our inadequacies to show us just how powerful He is. When He sends you, He equips you and makes a way just like in Matthew 15:35–39. When the apostles needed bread, God was the One who supplied it. Many people came to Christ on that mission including some people from my hometown, Pinsk, which was thousands of miles away from Siberia.

It was on the mission to Ukraine that I met Dr. Mark Eanes, an ophthalmologist. I didn't know at the time that it would be the first of many, many missions we would share, and I could not have imagined the bond we would develop over the years.

Grateful Children in China

I had the opportunity to go to China with Dr. Mark on two occasions with an organization called Gansu, Inc. This was very interesting because everywhere we went in China, we used a pop-up travel trailer, which had been converted into an operating room, allowing the ophthalmologists to perform cataract surgery in remote areas. Maria and I set up our clinic nearby, and throughout those two trips, we dispensed thousands of prescription glasses and reading glasses. Opportunities to share the gospel didn't come very often, but we were open about why we were there—to both show and share the love of God when and where we could. One of the things we used to start these

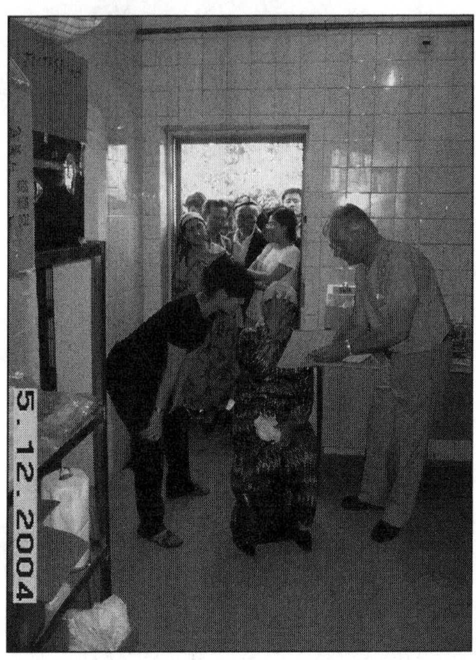

Bill testing the near-vision of a patient to dispense reading glasses. The pressing crowd waiting outside the door was too numerous to count and made going outside nearly impossible.

Children lining the walkway to welcome the doctors and optician to their school.

A welcome message written by school children in China.

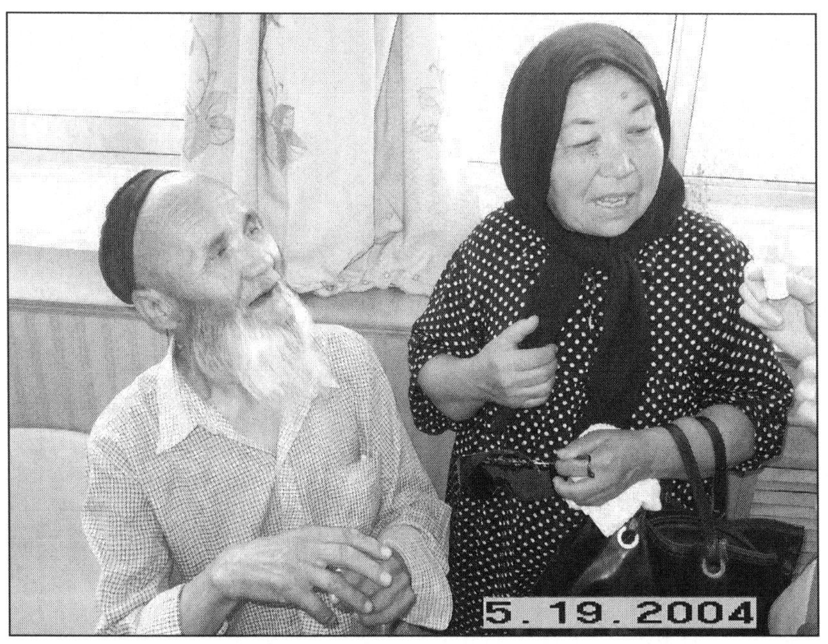

Husband and wife on the day after he recovered sight through cataract surgery, and she was successfully fitted with hearing aids

Bill, Maria, Dr. Mark, Jo, Dr. Lance, Debbie, and Heaven In Sight mission team (by the River of Jordan).

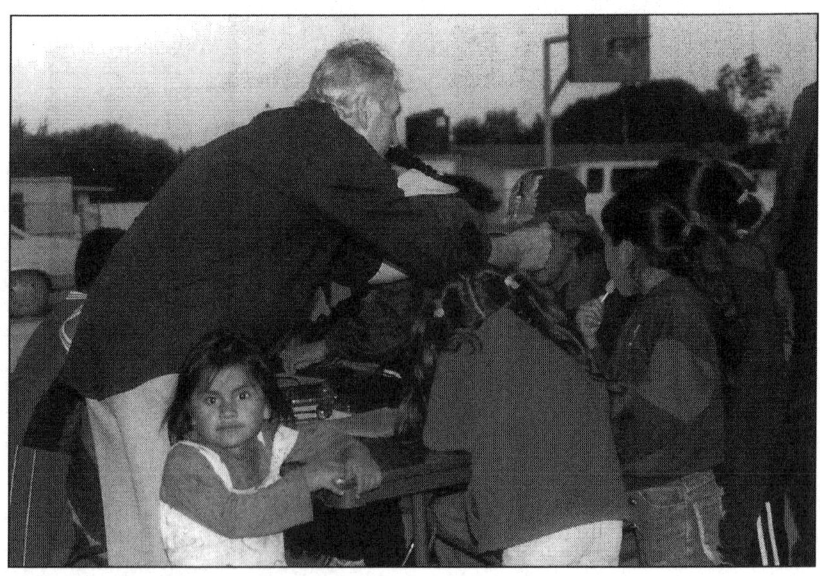

Bill with Heaven In Sight, fitting workers with glasses at a migrant camp in Vicente Guerrero, Baja, Mexico.

conversations were scriptures printed on reading material in a patient's native language. Rather than testing near-vision using random numbers and letters that decreased in size until they became a blur, the pages were full of Scriptures outlining the love of God and the gospel of Jesus Christ.

An unexpected blessing occurred during our trip to Turpan, China, in 2003. We usually dispensed glasses and did exams near the clinic site where our team was performing eye surgery. However, on this trip, one of our local translators made arrangements for us to go to some primary schools in the area, which we did several times toward the end of our workdays. What a huge surprise to see these children lined up along the street, clapping and waving small flags to welcome us to the school! Dr. Mark would do a quick refraction of the children's vision and, sure enough, we not only had glasses in the correct power, but many of the frames that had been given to us (in the miraculous story in Chapter 12) fit these little children perfectly. We had just the right number of boys' and girls' frames. Most of these children had never worn glasses and were so happy to see clearly for the first time! Once again, God showed His perfect plan in the donation of these children's glasses years before this mission.

We have been blessed to serve alongside Dr. Mark and Dr. Lance and their wives, Jo and Debbie (both nurses). There has never been a dull moment in this group, and I am very grateful for the God-ordained friendships in our lives. By the time Dr. Mark founded Heaven In Sight, we had already traveled many miles together on the Flying Hospital, Operation Blessing/CBN, and Gansu Inc.

CHAPTER FOURTEEN

An Honor and a Blessing

I will bless those who bless you, and whoever curses you I will curse; and all peoples on earth will be blessed through you.

—Gen. 12:3

To the Jew First

We began traveling with Jewish Voice Ministries International (JVMI), a messianic Jewish organization, in 2005 and would eventually volunteer on more than 25 medical missions and/or festivals. The mission of JVMI is to share the good news of the gospel with all people—to the Jew first, and then to the gentile (as commanded in Romans 1:16). Specifically, their heart is to locate and minister to the "lost" tribes who have been scattered throughout the nations, including holocaust survivors. We have seen God do many miraculous things in Addis Ababa, Woliso, Gondar, and Hosanna, Ethiopia; Mposi and Buhera, Zimbabwe; Manipur and Mizoram, India; and many, many sites in Israel. JVMI's ministry is multi-faceted. While this is not an all-inclusive list of countries or missions they have undertaken, JVMI has also established many messianic Jewish congregations, including 50 in Zimbabwe and 18 in Ethiopia (as of 2017). It has been a blessing to travel with JVMI and an honor to share the love of *Yeshua* with God's people while ministering to their needs.

One of my favorite memories with JVMI is from a mission trip to Manipur, India, where we set up and operated out of a large church. A father brought his son to us, carrying him on his back because the boy's legs did not work at all—they just dangled uselessly. He told us the boy had fallen from a tree many years ago and since that time he had not been able to walk. He had not been able to speak or see very well either, and these things kept him from being able to do well in school. Dr. Lance Haluka examined him and determined that he needed glasses badly, so we found eyeglasses that would fit. He saw well with the glasses and he was very, very happy! Lance, Maria, and I prayed for the boy, and then we suggested he go to the prayer room. Again, the father put the boy on his back, and they headed off in the direction of the Prayer Room for prayer and to minister to their spiritual needs.

One of JVMI's most impactful ministries is the "Prayer Room," and you will find one on every campus of every medical mission. Everyone who passes through the compound or receives services of any kind is encouraged to visit there, and most do. In these prayer rooms, tens of thousands have come to know the Lord; countless miracles have occurred; and many, many Bibles have been distributed.

> *And the apostles said unto the Lord, Increase our faith.*
>
> —Luke 17:5 (KJV)

About an hour after we sent the boy and his father to the prayer room, patient flow in the optical room slowed down. I asked Dr. Lance if he would stay in optical for a little while, so I could take a walk and stretch my back. I decided to go down the stairs to the main open area of the clinic when I saw a boy running up and down the steps. I thought for a minute he looked like the boy we had prayed for earlier, but I convinced myself this could not be, and I turned away and kept walking.

One of the workers from the church stopped to ask me where I was from and what I did. While I was having a conversation with the worker, I felt someone tug on my lab coat. I turned around to see who was trying to get my attention and, sure enough, the boy we had prayed for and his father was standing there. They had pure joy on their faces! And as if that was not miracle enough, I was even more shocked when the boy took off the eyeglasses we had given him and handed them back to me. In my heart, I knew what had happened, but I had to ask, "What is wrong with them?" He told me there was nothing wrong—he could see, he could walk, he could talk—God had healed him! He simply did not need the glasses anymore. There are no words that can describe the feeling that came over me. We cried and praised God for what He had done and what He can do.

> *You will say then, "Branches were broken off so that I could be grafted in."*
>
> —Rom. 11:19

Over the years there have been many other occasions when we fit glasses or hearing aids and people came back the next day to give them back to us because God had healed them, so they were no longer needed. There is no way to remember or tell all the things He has done.

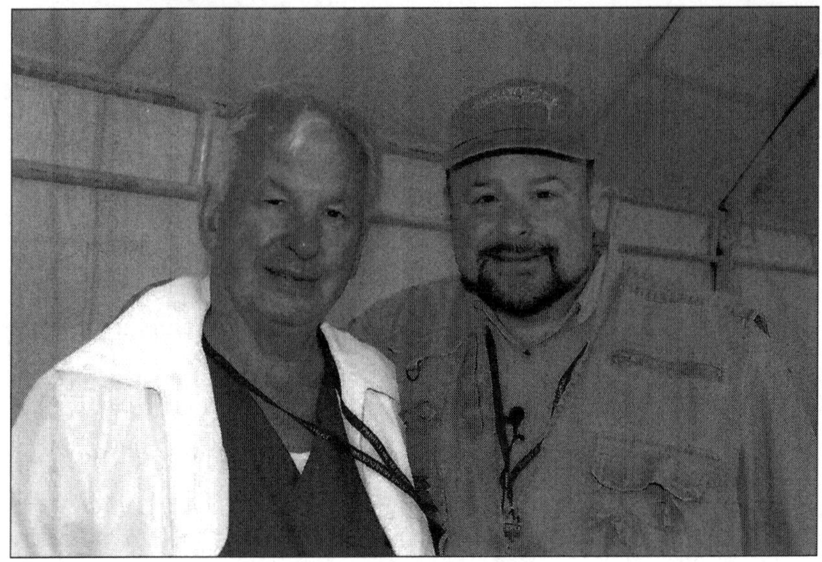

Bill (left) with Rabbi Jonathan Bernis, President and CEO of Jewish Voice Ministries International.

There is no less joy in the miracles like these that we have experienced in recent years than the first. Sharing them never gets old. We are commanded in the Scripture to tell of the miracles we have seen, and that is what I have tried to do.

> *O give thanks unto the LORD; call upon His name: make known His deeds among the people . . . talk ye of all His wonderous works.*
>
> —Ps. 105:1 and2b (KJV)

I pray that you will have as much joy in service to our Lord as Maria and I have experienced in our life. Sure enough, you will be able to look back and see how the trials, the joys, and the stories in your life have served to spare and prepare you for His service.

PART II

Maria Wojtaszewski née Kubacki

Who can find a virtuous woman? For her price is far above rubies. The heart of her husband doth safely trust in her, so that he shall have no need of spoil.

—Prov. 31:10–11 (KJV)

CHAPTER FIFTEEN

A Difficult Childhood

The Spirit of the Lord is upon me, because he hath anointed me to preach the gospel to the poor; he hath sent me to heal the brokenhearted, to preach deliverance to the captives, and recovering of sight to the blind, to set at liberty them that are bruised.

—Luke 4:18 (KJV)

I was born in Poland in December 1937 before World War II began. I was very young when my dad was drafted into the army, and my mother was left alone to care for my little sister, Christa, and me. We were forced to leave the country with only the few things we could carry in our hands. I remember Mom carried diapers and a down feather bed for my sister to sleep in. However, before we could leave Poland, my sister developed a whooping cough. Mom took her to the hospital, but there was no one to take care of me so she could not stay with her. Each time my mother went to see her at the hospital, I had to be left, crying and alone, outside the entrance gate. If that was not bad enough, every time my mother visited, she found my sister lying on a cold cement floor, and sometimes she was almost blue from lack of oxygen. She was getting worse, so my mother decided to take her home.

It was late November and very, very cold when we escaped to Germany, and my sister continued to get worse. Hoping that

Dad would be able to find us, Mom left the details of where we planned to go with other family members. Months passed. Mom was not getting much rest between providing for and taking care of my sister and me. Some of our new neighbors said she should just let my sister die. They warned her that if she died, there would be no one left to take care of me. Mom would not hear of it! Looking back, I don't know how she survived all the worries and physical demands of taking care of two children, escaping the country, and especially the loneliness. Finally, my father found us and we were reunited.

A few years later my mom became ill and she was told she had gallbladder stones. She became so ill that for many days, she could not even get out of bed. My dad took a job as a carpenter in Hanover, which was a few hours away from where we lived. He came home by train as often as he could to give my mother whatever money he could, but he was not able to stay home and care for her. That is when my mother called me into her room and taught me how to make a fire in the old stove and cook oatmeal for my sister and me. We did not always have the ingredients for everything we *wanted* to eat, but God always supplied and sustained us.

Our lives were hard. We had to learn the German language, and we were not welcomed there. We were stoned, we were spat on, and we were called very ugly words. Through all this, God was with us. Sometimes, we saw bullets flying everywhere, and there were even times we had to leave the house to find hiding places. One night we escaped to a brook which, I am sure seemed a lot bigger than it really was. My parents told us to grab a bush, hold on tight, and not to move. I remember crying to my parents that I was afraid I could not keep holding on; I thought I would fall

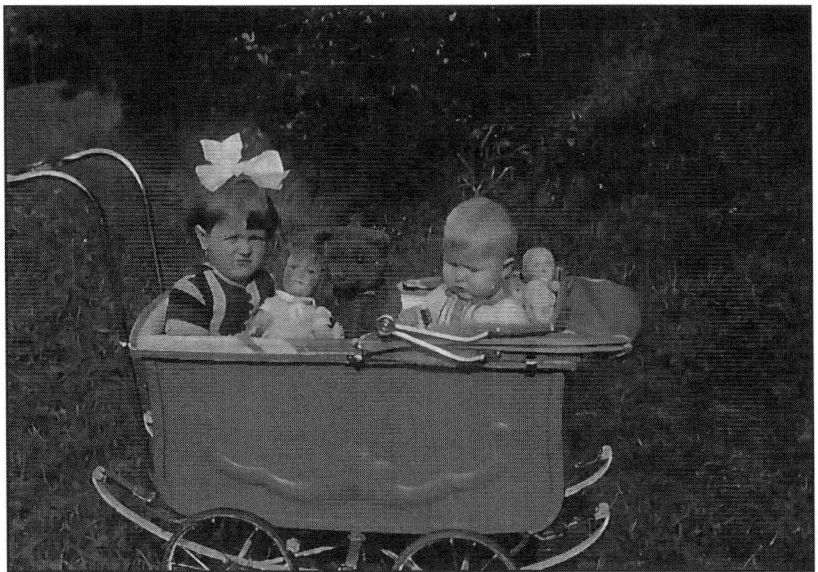

Maria (left) and her little sister, Christa (right).

into the water and drown. They reassured me they would save me if I fell. On another occasion the American planes were flying over, looking for soldiers. They came down very low over the hills that we and a few other young families had hidden behind. The mothers who had babies took diapers and waved them like flags to show the bombers that we were only families, hoping they would leave us alone. In tough times, God is always there. He said He will never leave us nor forsake us.

CHAPTER SIXTEEN

A Child of God

Since my youth, God, you have taught me, and to this day I declare your marvelous deeds.

—Ps. 71:17

My mother came from a Christian family. She, herself, was not a Christian but she remembered the prayers and seriousness of the people who believed in God, and she understood the importance of living a godly life. She remembered that on one occasion a pastor announced they would be having communion, but someone had a fight with their spouse before coming to church. The pastor told them it would be wrong to participate in communion without seeking forgiveness first. This caused my mom to reverence God and understand what He could do.

Growing up we had been told we were Catholic, but Mom stayed neutral. One day missionaries came to our little town of Odagsen to preach and to help in any way they could. They spoke neither German nor Polish; they were Ukrainian. At this point, the question may come to mind, "Why is it necessary to give money to or endure the inconveniences and hardships of missionaries in a foreign country?" I will *forever* be grateful to God for those missionaries. Mine was a difficult soul to win, and I can tell you, the enemy did not like this soul forsaking him for Christ.

> *And everyone who has left houses or brothers or sisters or father or mother or wife or children or fields for my sake will receive a hundred times as much and will inherit eternal life.*
>
> —Matt. 19:29

Living the life God wants us to live is not always easy. We had meetings at my aunt's home, but my father would never allow us to have meetings at our house. Eventually, he would not even let us go to our aunt's house or anywhere else meetings were being held. One day a preacher from a nearby city came and announced that we would be having water baptism. I was so excited and could not wait to be baptized, but the preacher told me I needed to go to my father and let him know what I planned to do. (I was still a minor at that time and needed permission.) I knew how my dad felt about it, so I told the preacher he needed to be there with me when I asked for permission. This made the enemy upset, for sure. The pastor came and told my dad that I wanted to be baptized and that it should be my decision, not his. I watched as he started to shake, and he screamed at the preacher, "She was born a Catholic and will die a Catholic!" I tried to tell my dad that I found God and that *He* had saved me, not the Catholic church or anyone else. I told him I could never fail God. I told him, "Even though you are my father and it is important to obey you, God is greater to be obeyed." He picked me up and threw me across the room and said, "I will never let you have your way!" When one of our friends told us that my dad could get the police to stop the baptism, I was so disappointed; I thought I had no choice at that point.

Then I remembered a true story our pastor had told us of something that happened in Europe. It went something like this:

> A young girl was passing by a house one night when she heard beautiful music. She was so intrigued she stopped and went into the house where a group of believers was gathered, and there she gave her heart to the Lord. She left for home and she was so happy, but when she told her mother what had happened, her mom became angry and forbid her to ever go back. A few weeks passed and she felt she just could not stay away, so she decided to go back. When she returned home that evening her mom got furious again and yelled at her, "You disobeyed me, and you **will not** go there again!" This time her mother took an iron rod from the furnace and hit her over the head. The girl's head was split open and she was bleeding badly, but she looked up at her mother and said, "Mom, I am so sorry for you. I go to meet my Lord and Savior, and I will be happy, but I am so sorry for you," and then she died. When her mother realized what she had done and her father saw how genuine his daughter had been, they both repented and were saved along with all their neighbors!

So, I told myself I had done nothing wrong, and right there I promised God that I would serve Him all my life. It was then that I made up my mind to be baptized.

The day came when we gathered for the trip to the nearest swimming pool to be baptized, which was in the city of Einbeck. Odagsen was four kilometers distance from Einbeck, and the entire trip I was crying and praying and asking God to intervene in my situation. Imagine my surprise to see that my father had ridden his bike to the pool and was already waiting for me at the fence. We changed into our long white gowns and stepped into the water. Everyone who had been swimming in the pool got out of the water immediately, but they were very curious and stayed around to watch whatever was about to happen. We were baptized with my dad looking on. I passed by him at the fence as we left, and I told him I was sorry he did not understand why I was doing what I was doing. I told him I would be praying for him, and he just said, "It's all right."

We prayed for my father for many years after that, but it would not be until long after we came to America that he finally came to know the Lord. By that time, his children and children's children were praying for him. He prayed the sinner's prayer and accepted the Lord as his Savior two weeks before he passed. He had avoided one of my aunts for years because he did not want to be "preached to," but when he accepted Jesus Christ as his Lord and Savior, he called her immediately to tell her! My aunt already knew because she had a dream of him the night before in which he was surrounded by angels and was so very, very happy. God graciously assured us that my dad is with Him.

CHAPTER SEVENTEEN

Destiny Awaits - USA

Therefore shall a man leave his father and his mother, and shall cleave unto his wife: and they shall be one flesh.

—Gen. 2:24 (KJV)

Back to Germany. In 1955, we started the process of immigration to the United States of America. We were only a small handful of Christians in Germany, and when a missionary visited, he told us we needed to get to America as fast as we could. On December 4, 1955, we finally boarded the USS General W. C. Langfitt, and we arrived in the US on December 16, 1955. I was 18 years old. A nice family (the Parchuts) sponsored us through the Ukrainian church, which meant we had to learn both Ukrainian and English languages. Even before I learned English, I started working at a jewelry factory, Tessler and Weiss, in Union, New Jersey. It was two years later that Wasyl (Bill) and his sister, Katherine, came to work at the same factory. Wasyl and I were engaged in 1959 and set a wedding date for February 13, 1960. Apparently, this made the enemy upset again.

Wasyl moved with his parents to a farm in New Port, New York, and he was delivering milk to a dairy factory. One morning he climbed into his truck and had not left the farm far behind him when the truck malfunctioned. It overturned and he found himself upside down in a creek—truck and all. In the process of trying to get out of the truck, he cut his arm badly, all the way to the bone. He must have cut a main artery or vein because the bleeding was very bad, and he could not stop it. Fortunately, a neighbor (who also delivered milk to the same factory) came along and rescued him. He put Wasyl in his truck and took him into town, and from there a policeman took him to the hospital. The surgeon at the hospital said the arm would need to be amputated, but God saw it differently. One of the doctors intervened and said, "No, he may not ever use the arm again, but I will sew it together and see what happens." It took a while to heal, but he not only kept his arm, he regained full feeling and use of it!

December came, and it was my turn to get sick. I went to a doctor who told me I had a virus. I vomited for a few days and had a high fever, but when I found I could no longer move my left leg, we called the doctor. It was Christmas Eve, but he told us to go straight to the hospital where they discovered that I had a ruptured appendix. By that time, my fever was so high they refused to do surgery. There was no real cure for a condition as bad as mine at that time. My doctor went away to a physicians' meeting in New York where he "just happened" to meet a German doctor and shared my case with him. When my doctor returned home, he came straight to me and told me to put off the surgery for a few weeks. I followed his advice, and he started me on several antibiotics.

My wedding shower had been scheduled during this time and here I was, in the hospital, so it was canceled. I told the doctor we should postpone the wedding, but he said it would be okay to go ahead and have it, so we were married. Everyone had been praying, and God gave us the victory once again! There have been a lot of obstacles in our lifetime, but with His help, we have stood firm. The enemy does not win, and the devil is under our feet.

CHAPTER EIGHTEEN

God Calls, We Answer

And God is able to bless you abundantly, so that in all things at all times having all that you need, you will abound in every good work.

—2 Cor. 9:8

A Mission of Faith

It was not until many years later that God would call us to the mission field. We would have almost no money in our savings account, and we would encounter many trials along the way, but we would always trust God to supply our needs. Not our wants, but our needs. Through the years we have seen so many miracles that I cannot remember them all, but I would like to share a few of them with you.

One of my favorite testimonies about God's faithfulness involves a mission trip to Kazakhstan. It was about one week before we were scheduled to leave when our pastor asked if we had everything in order and were ready to go. We told him, "Not yet, but we will be." He was doubtful that we could obtain all the equipment and materials we would need in such a short time. We told him again, "We will have all we need. God will supply all our needs. He will not call us and then let us down; he knows all about us."

We had been invited to supper that night by one of the pastor's friends, and we went with him to the friend's home. His parents were missionaries from Kazakhstan, and it just happened that they were visiting. They had heard we were preparing to go to Kazakhstan and thought we might like to see some of their slide photos on a screen. Another friend who "just happened" to be an optician was also invited to the supper, and he struck up a conversation with Wasyl. The optician asked him if he had everything he needed for the trip and, naturally, he told him that we did not. The optician asked what he still needed, so Wasyl told him exactly what he needed, *not* what he wanted. The optician told him he had all that we would need in his cellar and asked Wasyl to come and get what he wanted. On the way home, the pastor asked if we enjoyed the Kazakhstani meal with lamb and so on. We told him we did enjoy the meal but even better, the optician had donated everything we needed for the trip. It had only been a few short hours before that he had asked if we had everything we needed! He just shook his head and said, "Wow, I can't believe it . . . you insisted you would have all you needed." We laughed, and I told him, "Oh ye of little faith!" So, we said we would never doubt God again.

This, of course, made the enemy even angrier, and he started to use fear for our children and things that might happen to them to intimidate us. We would not give in. We proclaimed that there is no other god than our God, and He is so good! Believe it. In this life, you will have trials, but with God there is hope. We found our joy in seeing people (both adults and children) being saved and seeing many other miracles. We saw deaf people hear, blind people see, and even lame walking because of God's touch on their lives. What a sight it was to see scores of people being touched as God passed over!

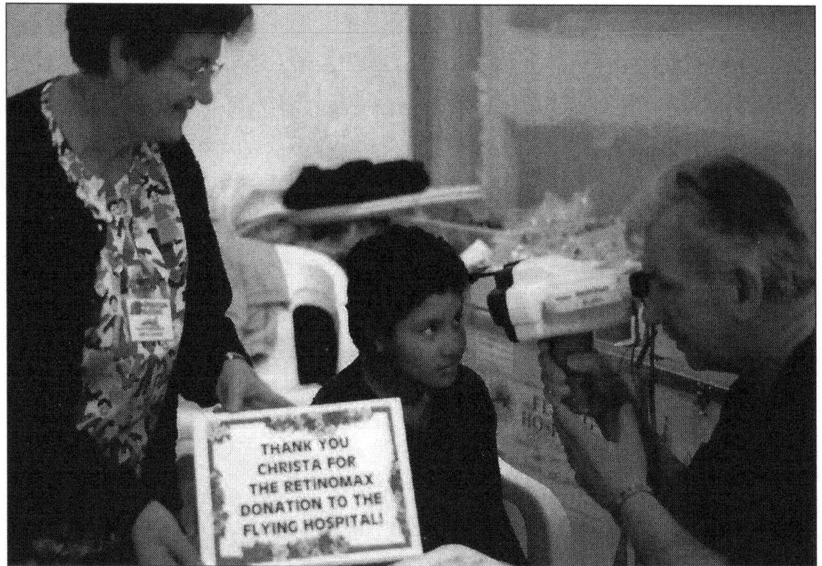

Acknowledging donations for much-needed equipment.

God Expands Borders

> *I will instruct you and teach you in the way you should go; I will counsel you with my loving eye on you.*
>
> —Ps. 32:8

I remember a trip to Kenya where we had set up the clinic in a church. (This is not unusual because sometimes the church is the best shelter and the cleanest place to have a clinic.) A man was brought to us; he was so blind he had to be led into the clinic by a friend. He had old broken glasses with very thick lenses, and he did not seem to be able to see any better with them than without them. I explained to him that we did not have any glasses that would cure blindness, but I would pray with him that God would give him back his vision. I also encouraged him to go through the prayer line and pray to accept the Lord as his Savior, and he would receive spiritual sight. He said to me, "If you can get me to see again, I will go to prayer and give my life to the Lord, *and* I will donate land to the church." I cleaned his lenses and placed them in a new frame and gave them back to him. Then we prayed for his vision. Suddenly, he looked up and then jumped to his feet exclaiming, "I can see again! I will go for more prayer and will be back tomorrow with my family. I will also bring the deed to my property to give to the pastor!" This property just happened to back up next to the church. It is no coincidence that the church had started a project to build a training center for pastors, so the land was much needed. One more time, God met the need.

Hope for the Hopeless

> *Whoever oppresses the poor shows contempt for their Maker, but whoever is kind to the needy honors God.*
>
> —Prov. 14:31

In 2002 we took a trip to Ternopil, Ukraine. It was during the winter, and there was a lot of heavy snow and ice. There was a poor family who had traveled on a train from very far away. It just so happened that my cousin from New Jersey visited a nearby orphanage regularly and had told them about the clinic. This family was so poor that the church had taken up a collection to pay for their fare to Ternopil. They arrived with only some fruit to share and a few sandwiches, so we fed them and put them up for the night where we were staying.

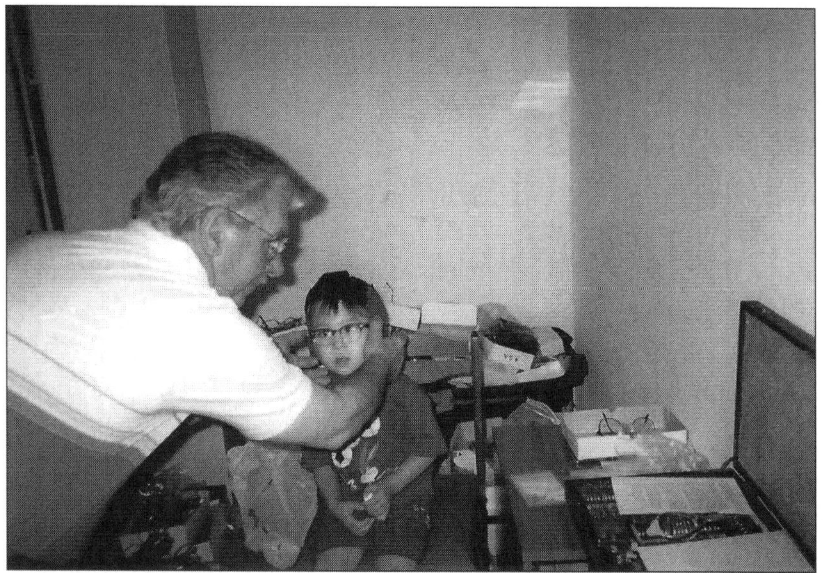

Bill fitting a young boy with glasses aboard the Flying Hospital while in Ukraine.

They brought a little girl with them who had a huge tumor on her head. She had such bad headaches she could hardly eat without getting violently ill, and as a result, she had lost a lot of weight. She had managed to get X-rays, and the doctors had told them there was nothing to be done for the tumor. They were also told that eventually her head would "split open," and she would die. When she was brought to the clinic, our doctors were in the hospital performing surgery and could not evaluate her, so we told them to return later in the evening. That night our neurosurgeon, Dr. Bert Parks, examined her. A surgical procedure was scheduled and although he told her that she would be fine, she still feared that she would die because of what the local doctors had told her. We prayed for her, and the surgery went well; the family was told to bring her back for a post-operative visit.

When the family returned the next day, they brought with them a little boy who was lame. They wanted our doctors to perform surgery on him as well. We were sad when we had to tell them there was no time left on the surgery schedule; our time had run out, and we were preparing to leave the country. Instead, everyone gathered around him and we prayed. He got up and walked and was healed! A year later, we visited my cousin for a birthday celebration. All the people in the community were so happy and grateful for what had happened the year before. They wanted to show their thankfulness by cleaning for us because there was no way they could pay us back. We assured them it was a nice gesture but that they should give God all the honor and glory because it was God who healed him, not our surgeons.

God's People, Our Privilege

> *"But I will restore you to health and heal your wounds," declares the Lord, "because you are called an outcast, Zion for whom no one cares."*
>
> —Jer. 30:17

In 2005, we were invited to travel with a well-known messianic Jewish organization called Jewish Voice Ministries International (JVMI). Our first trip was to Addis Ababa, Ethiopia, and it was the first of many trips we would take with JVMI. The ministry was to all who would come, but the mission was to share the good news of *Yeshua* (Jesus Christ) with the scattered Jews throughout the nations. It was very interesting to hear of some of the places the "lost" Jews had been found. The trip to Addis was a very long one. The mission there was to a very poor community of Jewish people, and we worked out of the home of a community elder,

Mrs. Zenovich. The Jews there were known as *Falashas*, which meant outcast people. At first, we had a problem because our equipment had been shipped ahead of us and had been held up in customs. (It is not uncommon for supplies and equipment to be held for ransom at airports; this has happened in many countries over the years.) We had limited materials to work with, but we were excited to see what God would do with what we had, and we managed until they eventually released the supplies.

A girl who was almost blind came to us, and we were able to give her strong glasses. She started jumping four or five steps at a time until her mother approached her, screaming, "She cannot see; she will get hurt!" But the daughter told her that she could see, and she was fine now! A 19-year-old young man was brought in with a doctor's note explaining that he was blind and there was nothing that could be done to help him. I agreed there was nothing we could do to help him, but we would pray with him that God would give him sight. We prayed and he said, "I can see something." Because there is always a long line of people waiting to be seen for eyeglasses, I suggested they go to the prayer room for more prayer, and he agreed. (JVMI always brings a group of counselors and prayer warriors who come for the specific purpose of praying for the needs of the people and the team members.) About a half-hour later, I went to the prayer room to find him sitting outside on a bench. He grabbed me and said, "Thank you! I am okay now, and I also found God!" In that community we saw deaf ears open, blind eyes see, and all kinds of sicknesses and disease healed. A multitude of people came to accept the Lord as their Savior, including priests and Imams. While we were there, healings and wonders and miracles were reported happening all over the country!

We took another very, very long trip with JVMI to Zimbabwe, Africa. This is a country full of witchcraft, but God was there to deliver them. They came with sickness and diseases—some even dying—but God was there to heal them. We had water baptisms, but most of all, salvations! Scores and scores of them.

Patients in line waiting to enter the clinic at Addis Ababa, Ethiopia.

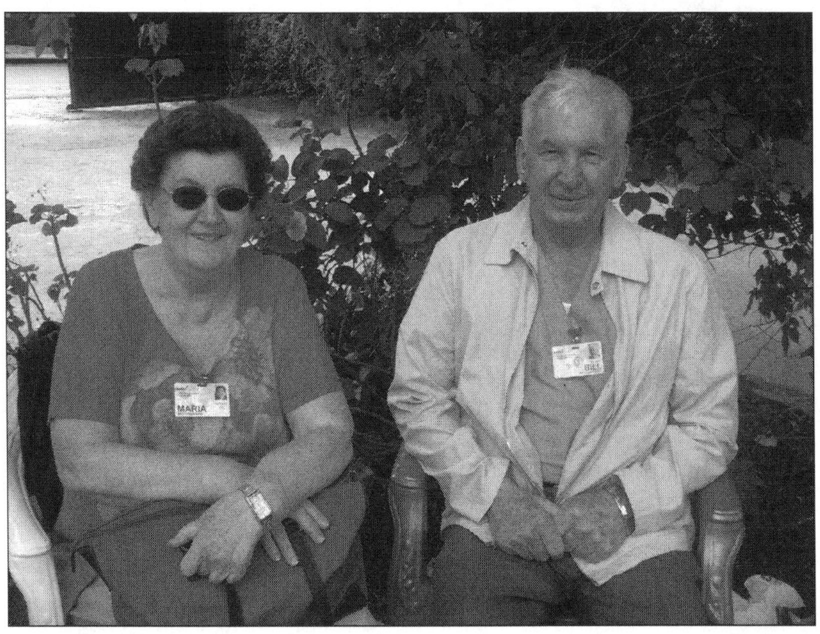

Maria and Bill at an outdoor gathering held by a local Messianic Jewish church in Addis Ababa, Ethiopia.

CHAPTER NINETEEN

"Challenges" on the Home Front

For our struggle is not against flesh and blood, but against the rulers, against the authorities, against the powers of this dark world and against the spiritual forces of evil in the heavenly realms.

—Eph. 6:12

All at Once

Sometimes things happen that we cannot control—bad things. God is faithful, and He always makes a way out . . . always! Before this book was finished, some bad things happened, and they just kept on happening. When the day came that I was diagnosed with cancer, it seemed like everything came together and turned into one big struggle. I knew in my heart that it was a spiritual one.

It had been a trying time for everyone. We were doing our best to deal with the Coronavirus pandemic—trying to stay healthy and wondering how safe it was to venture out from home, which masks to wear, and which "science" was or wasn't reliable. But when my sister passed away, I knew I had to go to Seattle for her funeral. On the way back home, I tripped in the elevator, hit my head, and had to take an ambulance ride to the emergency room.

After that, there were weeks of medical tests to find out how bad my injury was. I still had headaches and nausea, and the doctors feared the worst. CT scans and MRIs of my head didn't show bleeding or any other problems, but outside my skull was a different story. A golf ball-sized knot had formed on my forehead (which was actually a bruise, or collection of blood clots), and the blood drained from the bruise under my skin until it covered most of my face. It didn't seem to want to go away on its own, so the doctors decided to do a procedure to remove the blood. As the "knot" went down, my headaches went away, and I started to feel some better, but nausea persisted.

I began to have severe pain in my stomach. The nausea was making it hard for me to eat, so I had to go back to the doctor for *more* tests. This time I was diagnosed with gallstones and put on the schedule to have surgery. In the meantime, one of the test results showed a large "mass" that was sitting on the top of my stomach. The doctors refused to do surgery until they knew more about it, so the gallbladder surgery was canceled. Then came *more* tests.

> *And the peace of God, which transcends all understanding, will guard your hearts and your minds in Christ Jesus.*
>
> —Phil. 4:7

I knew in my spirit that it was cancer. I cannot explain the peace that God gave me at that time, and He continued to give me in the months after that. It was difficult for some people to understand when I would say things like, "If it is my time to go, God will take me, but if He's not done with me, He will help me to get better." Yes, there were still things I wanted to see come to pass in my family, but He gave me peace about those things too. He reminded me that He will accomplish His purposes whether I am on this earth or not. As the Apostle Paul wrote in Philippians 1:21, "For to me, to live is Christ and to die is gain." Maybe I would have to go through a long, hard time fighting this battle against cancer. Maybe I would enter into His presence and receive my eternal reward sooner than I thought. Either way, I knew He was with me, and His grace was sufficient for me just like He promised in 2 Corinthians 12:9.

No Coincidences

> *And who knoweth whether thou art come to the kingdom for such a time as this?*
>
> —Esther 4:14b (KJV)

Do you believe God has put each of us on this earth at a certain time, for a certain reason? We have many purposes, but it is up to us whether we will receive the blessings that come when we obey and do the things that He gives us to do. Dr. Mark Eanes and his wife, Jo, became, even more, a part of our lives during this time. We had served on the mission field together for so many years, and Dr. Mark would always say, "Maria, you have ministered to so many people across the world; it's time for someone else to help *you.*" Dr. Mark and Jo made many trips to the cancer center with us, using their medical knowledge to explain what the doctors were telling us, and then explain to the doctors what was difficult for us to say. It just so happened they were not working at the time, and they could not go on mission trips because of the pandemic. I now know that those things were because of God's timing, and He was using them to accomplish His will. I understand that God put them in our lives "for such a time as this."

We live in a small town in South Georgia, but when I was diagnosed with cancer, we had been staying at our daughter's home in Tampa, Florida. Our daughter, Sharon, had several partial amputations of both her legs and the most recent one was not healing well. She was having a lot of pain– sometimes so bad that the medication would not even begin to relieve it. Some nights, all I could do was just hold her, and we would pray and cry together. Because her doctors were in Tampa, we decided to stay and care for her and take her to doctor appointments, physical therapy, and so on. We had been there almost a year when I got sick, and Bill had to take care of both of us. Dr. Mark and Jo drove from South Georgia to Tampa to go with me to my appointments at Moffitt Cancer Center, and they have been with me all along this journey. Our daughter, Cindy; my granddaughter, Christa; and my sister, Grete also came when they could. During this time, Sharon was fighting her own battles, and I was too weak to help her. Watching her suffer and not being able to help her was harder for me than everything else that was happening.

Strength to Stay the Course

I had all kinds of tests and procedures and chemotherapy treatments; then I developed atrial fibrillation. My heart rate and blood pressure were almost impossible to control. The more dehydrated I became, the worse it got. The more chemo I took, the more dehydrated I became. I couldn't hold down food or liquids, and I was very tired of hearing everyone say that I needed to eat and drink! These problems caused many trips to the emergency room and even a few hospital admissions as the doctors tried to get my heart rate and blood pressure under control. I even had a pacemaker implanted, but it didn't help much. I kept getting dehydrated, and the same thing kept happening all over again. During one of those hospital stays, we were able to schedule weekly IV fluid infusions as an outpatient, hoping I could avoid some of the hospital admissions. This seemed to help some. The bad case of shingles that came up on my left side didn't bother me that much because of everything else I was going through. In three months, I lost more than 40 pounds. I was unrecognizable compared to the person I had been six months earlier.

In March 2021, they told me I had less than one month to live, and the doctor mentioned that hospice care might be the best thing for me. I was so very tired, but again, I was at peace. My family became very upset at the thought of hospice and "giving up," and I assured them I would continue to do what was reasonable and leave the outcome up to God. If I was supposed to keep on fighting this battle, I knew He would give me the strength and grace to do it.

God Still Answers Prayer

As I write this, it is March 2022—one year since I was told I had less than a month to live—and they tell me I am in remission. I made pierogies today, and tomorrow I plan to go to my church. I have returned to my home, and I feel better every day. Sharon's wound has healed. She has been fitted with prostheses and continues to get physical therapy. She is planning a trip to Italy. To God be the glory! Let everything that has breath praise the Lord! If you have faith and believe, God can do anything according to His will.

I would like to stop here and thank everyone who has prayed for me and lifted up my needs to the Lord because he has kept me through these hard times. We have been blessed with so many friends and family, churches and mission organizations, and loved ones at home and throughout the world. I know God heard and answered their prayers.

His promises are not made to just a few; they are for everyone! He is there for you, waiting to be your Savior and meet all your needs if you will believe. Don't wait any longer. God is great, and heaven is real!

Thank you, again, for all your prayers.

CHAPTER TWENTY

Never Too Late

However, I consider my life worth nothing to me; my only aim is to finish the race and complete the task the Lord Jesus has given me—the task of testifying to the good news of God's grace.

—Acts 20:24

Is God Calling You?

There is no way to tell all the stories of all the things we have seen. We have been on over eighty mission trips all over the world since 1994, and God was with us everywhere we went! We are still not finished until Jesus tells us all that has been required of us is done. I have had people say they have seen angels behind us, and they came to see what they were doing. We have seen God provide what we needed through miracles, and we have seen Him use other people to do it. We could not have done it on our own without the obedience of so many who have provided physical or spiritual support.

Thank you, Operation Blessing and Jewish Voice Ministries International. God bless you mightily even more than He blessed us!

We thank God for meeting Dr. Mark Eanes (Heaven In Sight Ministries) and Jo Eanes, his wife, who was willing to give up her time to type the book that we dictated. They were always there for us; they are very generous people, and we love them as our own family. We cannot express all our love for them.

Also, our friends, Dr. Lance Haluka and Debbie. We met Dr. Lance in Kenya in 2000 and since that time, they have become our family too. They always encourage us.

We have met and served with lots and lots of people who are our friends, those we love and pray for and cherish. There is no way to list them all, and there is no amount of money that could repay them, but God sees and knows who they are.

We would never have thought about writing a book, but our kids begged us to do it. They said it is not enough to just tell the stories because they might forget them. This way we can tell our children, grandchildren, and great-grandchildren about God's faithfulness. For our grandchildren Kirsten, Michael, Chantal, and Christa; our great-grandchildren Samuel, Jameson, and Madison—it is our hope you will enjoy reading this book one day.

If you think God may be calling you to be a missionary, my advice is to pray about and seek His timing. You will see His provision in ways that you could never accomplish on your own. Sometimes, you may say, "Ouch!" and sometimes you may say, "Oh, that is so good!" but through all of it, the praise goes to our Lord and no other. We have seen God do so many mighty things that no man could ever do, and once you taste His glory, you will never be the same. We have had our "ups and downs," but looking back, we would not change a thing.

It would take more than one book to record all we have seen over the years. As the song says, *"To God be the glory, great things He has done."*

He Will Bring It to Pass

I have tried to keep records of our travels since we began doing the work that we feel God has called us to do. I share this list to demonstrate that it is never too late to "get going." It doesn't matter how old you are or what talents you have, God can accomplish a lot with a little, in a short time. We have not traveled since the start of the Coronavirus pandemic and for other health reasons, but we hope to add more to the list, Lord willing. The dates and locations in the list below are accurate to the best of my knowledge:

1994	**Maladzyechna, Belarus** – Book of Life
1996	**Kiev, Ukraine** – Flying Hospital
1997	**Almaty, Kazakhstan** – Flying Hospital
1998	**Guayaquil, Equador** – Flying Hospital
	Brasilia, Brazil – Flying Hospital
	Recife, Brazil – Flying Hospital
	Cochabamba, Bolivia – Flying Hospital
	Hyderabad, India – Flying Hospital
	Krasnoyarsk Siberia, Russia – Flying Hospital
	Bratsk, Russia – Flying Hospital
2000	**Managua, Nicaragua** – Flying Hospital
	Pueblo, Mexico – Flying Hospital
	Kenya, Africa – Flying Hospital
2001	**Managua, Nicaragua** – Operation Blessing
	Danang, Vietnam – Operation Blessing
	Vicente Guerrero, Baja, Mexico – Operation Blessing

2002 **Ternopil, Ukraine** – Operation Blessing
Trinidad, Beni, Bolivia – Operation Blessing
2003 **Istalif Kabul, Afghanistan** – Operation Blessing
Phnom Penh, Cambodia – Operation Blessing
Vicente Guerrero, Baja, Mexico – Heaven In Sight
2004 **Turpan, China** – Gansu, Inc /Heaven In Sight
2005 **Addis Ababa, Ethiopia** – Jewish Voice Ministries International
Turpan, China – Gansu, Inc / Heaven In Sight
Vicenta Guerrero, Baja, Mexico – Heaven In Sight
2007 **Bethlehem, Israel** – Operation Blessing / Heaven In Sight
2008 **Bethlehem, Israel** – Operation Blessing / Heaven In Sight
2009 **Bethlehem, Israel** – Operation Blessing / Heaven In Sight
2010 **Mizoram, India** – Jewish Voice Ministries International
Manipur, India – Jewish Voice Ministries International
2011 **Manipur, India** – Jewish Voice Ministries International
Bethlehem, Israel – Operation Blessing / Heaven In Sight
Addis Ababa, Ethiopia – Jewish Voice Ministries International / Heaven In Sight
Addis Ababa, Ethiopia – Jewish Voice Ministries International / Heaven In Sight
Addis Ababa, Ethiopia – Jewish Voice Ministries International / Heaven In Sight
Woliso, Ethiopia – Jewish Voice Ministries International / Heaven In Sight
2012 **Woliso, Ethiopia** – Jewish Voice Ministries International / Heaven In Sight

Addis Ababa, Ethiopia – Jewish Voice Ministries International / Heaven In Sight
Gondar, Ethiopia – Jewish Voice Ministries International / Heaven In Sight
Manipur, India – Jewish Voice Ministries International

2013 **Manipur, India** – Jewish Voice Ministries International
Addis Ababa, Ethiopia – Jewish Voice Ministries International / Heaven In Sight
Gondar, Ethiopia – Jewish Voice Ministries International / Heaven In Sight
Mposi, Zimbabwe – Jewish Voice Ministries International / Heaven In Sight
Buhera, Zimbabwe – Jewish Voice Ministries International / Heaven In Sight
Hosana, Ethiopia – Jewish Voice Ministries International / Heaven In Sight

2014 **Israel** (multiple sites) – Jewish Voice Ministries International
Woliso, Ethiopia – Jewish Voice Ministries International

2015 **Woliso, Ethiopia** – Jewish Voice Ministries International
Israel (multiple sites) – Jewish Voice Ministries International

2016 **Israel (multiple sites)** – Jewish Voice Ministries International

2017 **Israel (multiple sites)** – Jewish Voice Ministries International

2019 **Israel (multiple sites)** – Jewish Voice Ministries International

After this I beheld, and, lo, a great multitude, which no man could number, of all nations, and kindreds, and people, and tongues, stood before the throne, and before the Lamb, clothed with white robes, and palms in their hands; And cried with a loud voice, saying, Salvation to our God which sitteth upon the throne, and unto the Lamb.

—Rev. 7:9–10 (KJV)

Conclusion

Sure enough, this is a book about miracles. It is a testimony of God's faithfulness in our lives. It tells about ministries that would never have been possible without God's miraculous intervention, and it tells of His love and compassion for needy people all over the world. It documents miracles of healing, and it testifies to thousands of salvations.

In the middle of all these miracles, we find ourselves wondering, *"Why me?"* Why did He miraculously spare *my* life so many times under so many impossible circumstances? Why does He trust *me* with "The Great Commission" of sharing His love and gospel with so many? Why does He allow *me* to travel all over the world and see His wondrous miracles among the multitudes? Most importantly, why did He love *me* enough to die for me so that I could be redeemed and spend eternity with Him?

We don't have all the answers, but this one thing we do know: God has not offered anything to us that He does not offer to *you* if you will only trust Him. He loves *you* so much that He died to spend eternity with *you.* He has a "great commission" for *you* to fulfill, a privilege that has been set aside *just for you* to experience—whether abroad or in your own neighborhood. And . . . Sure enough, God wants to do miraculous things in *your* life too!

We have been greatly encouraged with every trip we have made, and we have grown spiritually because we have realized and have seen *with our own eyes* how God keeps His promises. God is great! To Him be the glory.

About the Author

Wasyl (Bill) Wojtaszewski was born in Pinsk, Poland, in 1937—two years before the start of World War II. As a child, his journey through Germany during the war was not an easy one, but he and his family eventually migrated to Brazil where he was apprenticed as an optician and began his practice in San Paulo. Bill and his family eventually migrated to the United States in 1958, and his entrepreneurial spirit prompted him to open Lakes Optical Shop in Medford Lakes, New Jersey, where he practiced for 35 years. As an ordained minister in the Assemblies of God, Bill has served in a variety of ministries over the years, participating in more than 50 short-term medical/evangelical missions in 16 countries. He enjoys helping restore sight to underprivileged people groups around the world. This service provides access to many locations, some of which would otherwise be forbidden. His ultimate goal is to share the love of God and witness many souls receive spiritual sight. Bill is retired from his optical shop and lives in Lake Park, Georgia, near family and mission friends. He continues to do mission work as health and opportunity allow.

Heaven in Sight Missions is a non-profit, tax-exempt, non-political, charitable corporation dedicated to promoting and delivering eye care through glasses, surgery, and education throughout the world. Bill and Maria Wojtaszewski have been a huge blessing to the ministry of Heaven in Sight on numerous medical mission trips. As our in-person overseas projects have been slowed by travel limitations during the pandemic, we have searched for other evangelical outreach projects. This book is an excellent tool for reaching many with the hope and inspiration it can bring believers and non-believers who will place their trust in Jesus Christ.

MARK J EANES MD
Medical Director, Heaven in Sight